"This book is worth your time. ╵ ⟶ ⟶ ⟶
*to connect families to Jesus regularly through relationships and
experiences that will carry for generations. Years of experience in
leading successful ministries is brought together in an easy guide
to challenge pastors to have a long lasting impact on the families
they have been entrusted to lead."* ~ Dr. Leighton Flowers,
Director of Evangelism for Texas Baptists, Adjunct Professor of
Theology at Trinity Theological Seminary, Author of *"The
Potter's Promise: A Biblical Defense of Traditional Soteriology"*

*"Preston hasn't given ministry leaders just another program to
follow, but a strategy to implement. He writes from the passion of
honoring Christ and serving others by calling us to the 'Whom?'
and the 'Why?' Be ready, because Preston does not do our
thinking for us but rather challenges us, as ministry leaders, to
think and see how this strategy could fit in our ministry contexts
regardless of group size. This work is insightful, intentional, and
proven through a wealth of scripture. Preston is engaging in his
approach and you quickly realize he is on the same journey of
ministry as we are."* ~ Dr. Rusty Wheelington, Professor of Youth
Ministry, Leadership, & Christian Education at Howard Payne
University, Author of *"Ready: Recognizing and Responding to
God's Call"*

*"I have known Preston for many years and have had the privilege
of sitting on leadership boards with him several times. I only
know one thing to say about him: He truly loves the Lord and is
passionate about helping people meet Jesus, fall in love with
Jesus, and serve Jesus. I have served at his church on several
occasions and can easily see that this book is the fruit of a
thriving family ministry team. I personally believe every ministry
leader should read this book!"* ~ Billy Beacham, Founder &
President for Student Discipleship Ministries in Burleson, TX.
Co-founder of the See You At The Pole World-wide Student
Prayer Movement

"I first met Preston 10+ years ago while he was a coordinator for a National ministry. After only twenty minutes in conversation with him I walked away feeling like we had been friends for a long time. There is something unique about him. Over the past decade I have had the privilege of observing his ministry through mission partnerships and ministry opportunities. I have seen his heart for students to come to faith in Jesus and I have been able to see firsthand the fruit of this man's ministry. Perhaps best of all, I have had the pleasure of meeting many of his students personally and can clearly see that Preston lives the contents of this book. He is a practitioner of these principles. I wholeheartedly recommend Family Ministry That Counts!" ~ Dr. Bob Caldwell, Missions & Evangelism Pastor, The Ridge Church, Missouri. Director of One Team International, a student missions organization

"When given the opportunity, Preston will inspire the inner 'What if...?' in every conversation he has. True to his character, this book is exactly that kind of opportunity, inspiration, and conversation. Take your opportunity to think differently with this gifted 'What if...?' thinker and seasoned ministry leader." ~ Jason Richards, Director of Super Summer Evangelism Training Camps in Texas.

"Family Ministry That Counts is a must-read for every ministry leader. Preston Cave gives an easy to understand framework for your church's family ministry that clearly communicates, 'why we do what we do.' You need several copies of this book. One to keep and several to give to other ministry leaders!" ~ Bryan Hall, Student Pastor, Woodlawn Baptist Church, Austin, TX. Director for the Central Texas Youth Leaders Conferences

Family Ministry
That Counts

A fresh, simple approach to growing your
youth and family ministries through the
Gospel

Preston Cave

MinistryCue

Copyright © 2018 by Preston Cave
Ministry Cue Publishing
500 West Bluebonnet Dr. Granbury, TX 76048

www.ministrycue.com

Cover Design and Chapter Graphics: Brandon Cave

www.hellohealey.com

First Edition: October 2018
Printed in the United States of America
ISBN: 9781642543698

To my wife, Sarah Dee, and my kids Perry, Titus, and Parker, for always supporting and encouraging me to be a better person *as well as being* a better pastor. I love you!

Table of Contents

Acknowledgements

There have been so many people over the years pour into my life and ministry that I would never be able to name you all. So I feel the only appropriate thing to do here is acknowledge those who have had a direct impact on this project. I would like to thank Lakeside Baptist Church, and in particular Mark Forrest and Steve Quinn, for giving me a blank canvas to build a family ministry that has now become the contents of this book. Thank you to Dawn Weeks, Jim Horn, Brett Cook, Amy Nagel, and Gina Wilson, as well as the many staff and volunteers at Lakeside, for partnering with me to make this book a reality in the life of our Family Ministry. Thank you to Billy Beacham for your mentorship, Jane Wilson for your wisdom and coaching, Leighton Flowers for the many opportunities you've given me to serve, Jason Richards for the opportunity to serve with Super Summer evangelism training camps. These camps have shaped my life more than words could express. Thanks to Jimmy Storrie for the healing counseling at "StorrieHouse". To Dena Dyer for the first edits of this book and to the many pastors and ministry leaders that have read the rough drafts and shared their thoughts. To my brother, Brandon, for your friendship and for your help in the implementation process. To my mother Karen, and Terry, for always loving me and taking care of our family. To my sister, Lori, for believing in me when I didn't believe in myself. To Brandon and Karen Hixson for your lifelong friendship and for playing music together. Those were fun years! And to my personal prayer warrior, Betty Mitcham, for praying for me when I was a teenager and for many years of prayer even to this day. Thank you all! Lastly, thank you to my earthly father for showing me what God looks like and for always encouraging me to write a book. With all my heart, I wish you were here to read it.

When anyone in ministry talks about youth ministry or family ministry, I get excited because this ministry has meant so much to me as a new Christian since I came to Christ as a teenager, and now as a dad I am able to watch all six of my own kids grow spiritually because of their teachers, leaders, and youth pastors. As a pastor I believe kids and teenagers are a vital part of the life of a church. If a church doesn't do family ministry well, it can be disastrous for the health of a church.

Preston has done such a great job as our student pastor. He is a leader, a visionary, and loves students. I appreciate his approach to ministry and when I read his words in this book, it doesn't sound like a philosophy he has read elsewhere, but rather a reflection of his heart for ministry. The one purpose, two groups, three decisions, two priorities, and one person structure isn't a cliché or an ideal, it really is a way for students, parents, and leaders to know if they are making progress on the journey of discipleship.

Of course, it applies to every believer and ministry, so it is a good reminder for us all as we seek to not be distracted and fall for trying to please others, rather than the Lord. The real power behind this book is that it reminds us of how easily distracted we can get from the main thing. Although we all believe the main thing should be our focus, we fail to say no to the things we should say no to and say yes to the things we should say yes to. I think the Apostle Paul shared the same struggle in Romans 7. As you read *Family Ministry That Counts* you will discover some great wisdom that Preston has learned the hard way. How do I know? Many times I'm learning right alongside him. When I read books like this I always think, "I wish I had read this the day I began in ministry!" I'm amazed that we survived ministry with what little we knew in the beginning. That's a testament to the power of the Holy Spirit. Yet, we must commit to life-long learning to increase our capacity for ministry. Make sure that you don't skip the Appendices at the end. They are just as practical as the body of the book. My favorite is Appendix 3 entitle, "Unreached People Group." I told Preston I hope all of our leaders and parents take these principles to heart.

Many years ago when the church I pastored was building a new building, we had a capital campaign consultant come help us with our giving. He said that in all of his years of helping churches, the only time a church didn't succeed was when they weren't unified. What a concept! It's true with every aspect of church life. We all need to be reminded of what is important and all agree to keep these things at the center. The methods may indeed change, but one, two, three, two, one will remain until He returns!

Dr. Mark Forrest
Lead Pastor at Lakeside Baptist Church in Granbury, TX.

Let's face it. You're probably too busy to read this entire book. Do you know how I know? Because you chose to pick it up. Only busy people are attracted to a book cover that promises to simplify one's life. So yes, you're probably too busy to read this. But that's the very reason you should prioritize your week and start reading. I promise it will be worth it. But, just in case you get distracted, I'm going to give you the ending right now. So, here's the book in one sentence:

Our job, as ministry leaders, is to connect kids to Jesus daily, weekly, monthly, and yearly through intentional relationships and strategic experiences so that they can meet Jesus for the first time, fall more deeply in love with Him, and begin to serve Him in every area of their lives.

When we talk about connecting kids to Jesus daily, weekly, monthly, and yearly we have in mind the Connect Four Strategy that is further explained in the Appendix of this book. We also have a companion booklet called "Make it Count" that is designed to be generic and applicable to kids, volunteers, parents, and anyone else in your church. The goal is to help you develop a common vocabulary within your ministries by being able to give out these small booklets to guests and parents. In this way, you will be helping people better understand what your family ministry is all about.

I have decided to give you three unique reading experiences for this book. First, we encourage you to read the entire book from start to finish. Second, if you want to have an overview of the material, simply read the "Recap" section at the end of every chapter. There is also a section in the Appendix with the entire "Recap" sections in order for a fast, easy read. Third, you might desire reading the book from the end to the beginning. Start with chapter seven and read to chapter one. This is a model that works both ways.

For the remainder of this book, we will be looking at a model of ministry that is designed to become the infrastructure, or skeleton, of your ministry. This is NOT the meat. Too many churches have lots of meat (church programs) and no skeleton or philosophy. They have a table full of food, but no way of serving it effectively. People just walk up to the table and dive face-first into the meal. This becomes messy, and is a breeding ground for conflict. Some of the meat will spoil before being eaten, and other meat will have multiple people fighting over it like a bunch of rabid dogs. The breakdown/conflict/issue occurs because the leadership hasn't put a system in place to serve the meat.

Now, imagine having a structure in place to keep the meat better organized, a system to effectively serve the right meal to the right person at the right time. This philosophy is designed to be the skeleton of any ministry. It allows each church to choose which meats (programs) they want on the skeleton. The programs are secondary to the skeleton.

The Transferability of This Book

The principles found in these pages can be applied to a church of any size. I have been utilizing these principles most of my ministry, even when I was at a church with fewer than twenty kids. By applying these principles, I was able to see dramatic growth in that church, as well as in other places I have served. I understand that what our

Preschool ministry does is different than what our children's ministry and student ministry does. However, each of our ministries will have some aspects of a "big group" and a "small group" gathering. When I talk about "big group" and "small group," I realize some of you might be thinking, "My big group is actually a small group." If that's the case, start with the small group principles in this book and grow from there. Just know I started at a church with fifteen to twenty kids (on average) and was still able to apply the principles of the "big group" to my ministry.

I gathered the fifteen to twenty kids together for a "big group" experience, and we would worship together. Then, I encouraged them to get plugged into a "small group" in order to grow deeper in their faith. My "big group" had fifteen to twenty kids, and my "small groups" sometimes had fewer than five kids. The principles still worked.

Also, remember that family ministry is nothing more than the preschool, children, and student ministries all getting on the same page and no longer becoming separate silos within the church. We have found that when we all work together with a common vision we are able to get more done than we could independent of one another. The challenges faced in trying to write a book for every phase of ministry is that I sometimes use the terms "kids" or "child" to mean any student in the family ministry. I do not mean to speak down on teenagers by calling them children, so be sure you do not call teens kids just because I do in this book. Be appropriate at every phase of ministry. It is up to you and your team to wrestle with what parts of this book can be applied to your context. But don't feel like you cannot apply this book to your current setting simply because of the size of your church or family ministry. Take the transferable principles and apply them where you can. I believe the "skeleton" concept is transferable to a ministry of any size. Here is the skeleton we will spend the rest of our time together talking about. (Notice that this is a family ministry that counts...literally: 1..2..3..2..1!

Family Ministry Skeleton:

- One Purpose
- Two Groups
- Three Decisions
- Two Priorities
- One Person

A Tale of Two Ministry Leaders

The alarm rings out and it's time to get up for the day. Wayne slides reluctantly off the side of his bed and puts on his house shoes. He is so tired. He hasn't been sleeping very well. The thought of having to get dressed and go to work is more than he can bear. He takes his time getting ready for the day, and sluggishly heads out the door and off to work.

It has been a long time since the ministry brought him joy. Today, the sight of the church building drains the energy from his body. Wayne hates feeling like this. He remembers the excitement of ministry in his early years. There were long days back then too, but he was energized whenever he thought, "I can't believe they are actually paying me to do what I love!"

That feeling is long gone now. Wayne is more prone to feel underpaid than overpaid. It seems like there is always more ministry to do than there is time in the month. He can never get caught up, even though he hasn't t taken a day off in months. And the little bit of free time he does have is wasted by his lack of motivation and his desire to self-medicate (to help the day go by faster).

His ministry isn't healthy. His family isn't healthy. His relationship with God isn't healthy. And he begins to wonder what life would be like outside of ministry.

Then there is Bob. Bob actually woke up before his alarm sounded this morning and bounced out of bed. He has been doing that lately. He helps his wife get the kids ready for school; even making them breakfast, and then sees them off. He settles down with a nice cup of coffee and starts his daily "coffee break with Jesus." He has plans to finally read the Bible cover to cover for *enjoyment* rather than for sermon prep.

After reading a few chapters and spending time in prayer, Bob gets ready for the day. He can't wait to get into the office and finish planning for the next two months of ministry. He recently nailed down his sermon plans for the spring semester, and he's excited about the potential of some of his student leaders. God has blessed his ministry with kids discipling other kids. He can't stop thinking about how cool it is to see the passion in their faces as they pour out their lives for one another.

Bob has a few more tasks to complete on his to-do list before enjoying a few days off. He has several "honey-do's" to complete on Saturday before the weekly family grill-out, so he's finishing his work today in order to focus on his family this weekend. Bob scurries out the door, drives to the church, and thinks to himself, "I can't believe they pay me to do this!"

His relationship with God is healthy. His relationship with his family is healthy. His ministry is healthy.

Maybe you can relate to Bob. Maybe you can relate to Wayne, but wish you could relate to Bob. Both of the scenarios above are from my life and ministry at one time or another. They are an exact description of how I have felt. This is why I have decided to write this book. I remember being so burned out I literally questioned my self-worth. And I lost a lot of sleep. I never want anyone else to experience what I experienced during my lowest points in ministry. So, hopefully this book will be a breath of fresh air for you as you prayerfully consider which parts to apply to your life and ministry.

In his book, *The Power of Habit[1]*, Charles Duhigg shares that habits can be formed when we set up specific cues to point us towards a certain routine. If one wants to develop the habit of Bible reading, he or she will need to set up a regular "cue" (such as a notification reminder on their phone) to remind them to read. The process looks like this:

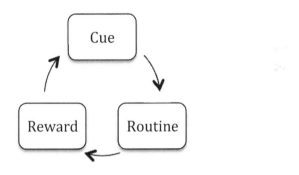

A specific cue moves us towards a certain routine. The routine gives us a special reward. The reward encourages us to complete the routine the following day. However, you need the same specific cue in order to remind you to do the routine. This theory/practice can also help us stop bad habits. If we want to stop eating junk food, we need to identify the "cues" that make us crave junk food. Sometimes we can just change or take away the cue, and the routine will disappear. But often times the cue is a regular part of our day, such as 3 p.m. If we can identify the cue, we can prepare ourselves for it and actually use the established cues to help form new routines--with a similar reward. In ministry, the reward is leading and discipling people towards Jesus. But what is our routine for helping change lives? And what is our cue?

Most of the time we get our cues from our pastor, boss, parents, or denominational leaders. Nothing is wrong with learning from these people, and I would always encourage submitting to the authorities above you. But let me ask you a question: when was the last time you simply prayed to God asking Him for the vision for your ministry? I pray this book will encourage you to get your *cues* from King Jesus, and that you will see the importance of developing an effective ministry *routine* to help accomplish the vision God has given you. The REWARD is too important for us to miss our CUE!

Conclusion

I could think of no better story to tell as we introduce this book than the opening story from *"Spiritual Disciplines for the Christian Life"* by Donald Whitney.

> Imagine six-year-old Kevin, whose parents have enrolled him in music lessons. After school every afternoon, prompted by his mother, he slouches into the living room and strums songs he must practice--but doesn't like--while watching his buddies play baseball in the park across the street. That's discipline without direction. It's drudgery.

> Suppose an angel visits Kevin one afternoon during guitar practice. In a vision, he's transported to Carnegie Hall. He's shown a guitar virtuoso giving a concert. Usually bored by classical music, Kevin is astonished by what he sees and hears. The musician's fingers dance on the strings with

fluidity and grace. Kevin thinks of how stupid and clunky his own hands feel when they halt and falter over the chords. The virtuoso blends clean, soaring notes into a musical aroma that wafts from his guitar. Kevin remembers the toneless, irritating discord that comes stumbling out of his.

But Kevin is enchanted. His head tilts to one side as he listens. He drinks in everything. He never imagined that anyone could play the guitar like this. "What do you think, Kevin?" asks the angel. The answer is a soft, slow, six-year-old's "W-o-w!" The vision vanishes, and the angel is again standing in front of Kevin in his living room. "Kevin," says the angel, "the wonderful musician you saw is *you* in a few years." Then pointing at the guitar, the angel declares, "But you must practice!" Suddenly the angel disappears and Kevin finds himself alone with his guitar.

Do you think his attitude toward practice will be different now? As long as he remembers what he's going to become, Kevin's discipline will have a direction, a goal that will pull him into the future. Yes, effort will be involved, but you could hardly call it drudgery.[2]

Perhaps you are at a point like I was several *tears* ago...oops...I mean several *years* ago. Maybe you viewed your ministry as drudgery. This story should encourage us to refocus our eyes, not on what *IS,* but on what *COULD BE.* I believe, as Dr. Barry St. Clair would say, "It is important to always keep the main thing the main thing, and Jesus is the main thing!" When we lose sight of the main thing, life and ministry will slowly begin to feel like drudgery. However, with direction comes clarity. Clarity frees us to be creative. Creativity allows us to act within the divine nature we were created. Divine image-bearing breeds passion. Passion leads to fulfillment. And fulfillment brings peace. Do you want peace? If so, keep reading.

Introduction

13

ONE PURPOSE
CHAPTER 1

I remember sitting in a circle with a group of ministry leaders discussing the future of church ministry and different challenges ministry leaders face today. One of the men looked at the group and simply asked, "So, can somebody tell me exactly what this 'family ministry' thing is all about?" There was silence for a few moments. Then we began discussing what a family ministry might look like in our churches. This experience helped me see that, even though "family ministry" models have been around for a while, many people are still having trouble wrapping their minds around thinking about *church* in a different way.

Perhaps your church is in the same place right now and you feel like you should move towards a family ministry model, but you aren't really sure what that means. Well, before we get started with the practical side of family ministry let's talk for a moment about what we mean by "family ministry" and what it is all about.

From my perspective family ministry is not very difficult to understand, once you watch a 400-meter relay race. In this race you have four runners, each sprinting a 100-meter lap and then passing the baton to the following runner. The fourth runner is the one to finish the race. I want you to picture the preschool ministry as the first runner in the relay race. Their job is to establish a solid trust foundation in the life of your babies, toddlers, and parents in order to begin the process of discipleship. They will then pass these toddlers off to the children's ministry, where the goal will be to introduce the kids to the Gospel story and other bible stories, thus building upon the foundation laid by the preschool ministry. When a preteen gets to middle school the children's ministry will successfully "pass the baton" of discipleship on to the middle school (MS) ministry. The MS ministry is tasked with helping affirm the preteens and helping them navigate through the process of adolescence (we'll talk about this later). Once a student enters ninth grade the MS ministry passes the "baton" to the high school (HS) ministry to continue the process of discipleship that started with the preschool leaders. By the way, no respectable HS minister will walk around believing they are the sole reason their students are spiritually mature. A good HS minister always understands that any success they have in their ministry is often due to the foundation laid by, and the discipleship of, the ministries prior to HS.

This all takes place with a fresh understanding that ministry to kids is not the main goal of church ministry. "Family ministry" is different from past ministry models in that it is a paradigm shift from viewing our jobs, as ministry leaders, as partners to the *whole family* and not just to the *kids* in our care. The challenge for many churches today is that they are already set up for "family ministry", yet they have each ministry (runner) on a separate track running in a different race. There is no synergy among the ministries and, therefore, no common strategy for discipleship. Thus, the fruit of ministry is dwarfed simply because there is no system in place to manage and create growth. Family ministry, then, is the church's attempt to get every ministry on the same page in order to run the "race" together. The family ministry model also recognizes that what happens at the church is important, but what happens at home is even more important. So, partnering with parents is not just a suggestion, it is a necessity.

For better or worse, what happens at home is more impactful than what happens at church.

The first thing any church must do in order to develop a successful family ministry is to get on the same page with a purpose. For the remainder of this book we will be looking at a purpose statement that can be adopted by your church or modified in any way you'd like. This is my church's family ministry statement and I like how clear it is. However, if you'd like to work on your own purpose statement feel free to use the worksheet in the Appendix of this book as a guide for your team.

One Purpose

Connecting Kids to Jesus Daily, Weekly, Monthly, and Yearly

Life is hard. Add a second life to that and it gets even more challenging. This is why so many marriages fall apart. Now add little rug rats into the mix, and it is amazing the family unit is still in existence. You see, we were created in the image of God from the beginning. But something went terribly wrong. Man sinned--and sin broke God's perfect creation. From the time sin entered the picture, every birth has resulted in the production of a broken person. Broken people only have one option: marry other broken people and have little broken children. And the result is a world of family units comprised of broken people. As we join one family unit to another the result is the best reality show on television. No wonder we have so much conflict in our churches. Think about it. We have one messed-up family hanging out with dozens or hundreds of other messed-up families in the melting pot called church. Why are we surprised when things go wrong? We should be surprised when things go right. Ministry, then, is our attempt to resource and rescue the hurting and broken family from certain discord and dysfunction. Herein lies the problem:

Pastors are also broken people with broken families trying to stay afloat in this broken world.

Pastors are just broken people leading other broken people to God's repair shop. But if we were honest, we would admit we really have no idea where to start. Just like life is hard, ministry is hard too. Every person is in a different stage of life, moving at different speeds, and at a different place in their spiritual journey. And for many of us ministers, we are trying to figure out this thing called life too. Yet we are expected to help others even though we often need help ourselves.

Ministry is hard. But what if ministry wasn't that hard to *understand*? What if there was a simple litmus test we could use to determine whether we were truly making a difference for the kingdom? What if we didn't feel we had to neglect our families for the sake of others? What if there was a model of ministry that ministered to the ministry leader as well?

When we boil everything in Christianity down to the bare bones we can see it. Ministry is not as complicated as we make it out to be. Ministry is about helping people connect to Jesus. It's more than hosting successful conferences. More than building massive facilities. Even more than *preaching*. Our job, as ministers, is to help people connect to Jesus. Now, before you crucify me for underplaying preaching let me explain: the purpose of preaching is also to help people connect to Jesus.

C.S. Lewis once said,

> *"In the same way the Church exists for nothing else but to draw men into Christ, to make them little Christs. If they are not doing that, all the cathedrals, clergy, missions, sermons, even the Bible itself, are simply a waste of time. God became Man for no other purpose."*[3]

C.S. Lewis would say that even the Bible is a waste of time *IF* it does not lead people to Jesus. What a statement! Let's look at Jesus for a moment. His entire ministry circled around being with his disciples and having them follow him. Even the Apostle Paul shared this vision when he said in 1 Corinthians 11:1,*"Follow* my example as I *follow* the example of Christ." (Emphasis mine)

Jesus spent some time on this concept in John 15 when he talked about fruit. His entire premise in John 15 was to help the hearers understand their responsibility in staying connected to Him. Only through Jesus could the fruit of his ministry be revealed. And if we, as leaders, can connect kids to Jesus then our ministries will be more fruitful as well.

The whole Bible, from start to finish, is one giant story of God redeeming man back to himself through the person and work of Jesus Christ. God created the world and formed man from the dust of the ground. God then breathed life into man. God gave him a command – rule. Rule over the fish of the sea and the birds of the air and over every living thing... God said RULE. Adam and Eve forfeited that right when they ate the fruit. God still wanted to have a people rule on his behalf. So he selected one man, Abraham, and through Abraham selected a nation to be his Holy people - the children of Israel. Time and time again, God's people rebelled against him, so God finally chose to put on flesh and make his dwelling among us in order to live the life we could not live. The stories of the Old Testament point to this moment.

Leading up to the New Testament, the children of Israel were waiting expectantly for a new King to restore the glory of what once was in the kingdom of David. They called this man the Messiah - anointed one - KING! But when the true Messiah, King Jesus, came they did not receive him. Instead, they put him to death by nailing him to a cross.

As we understand the story of God in history (God redeeming man BACK to himself) and who Jesus is in that story; namely, the resolution of the story of the Old Testament, then we will better grasp our role in that story. We are simply storytellers of HIS story.

This may seem like it should go without saying, but *Jesus* is the main character of God's story. Not us. As ministers of this Gospel story, it is our job to help people follow *Jesus* and not us. But there is an epidemic in ministry today. It is the problem of narcissism. Too many ministry leaders have become codependent on the kids they serve. Many ministry leaders find their identity in the number of people that need *them*.

Kids do this with social media all the time. They place self-worth on how many followers they have or how many reactions they receive from a certain selfie. But remember, we are not called to be like the people we serve. We are called to be *in* the world, but not *of* the world. However, just like the kids they work with, many leaders use followers as a sign of importance. Because of this, the ministry is more about leading kids to the ministry leader than it is about leading them to Jesus.

It should NEVER be about leading kids to the ministry leader! It is ALWAYS about leading kids to Jesus.

Many years ago, I was so convicted of this that I wrote a prayer in the front of my Bible that I try and pray every time I speak or serve. I encourage you to adopt it for your ministry, as well. Here is the prayer:

God, you have given me the opportunity to influence a generation. May I be faithful and effective to lead them to you and not to me. Give me more opportunities soon.

We need a new generation of leaders who won't find their identity in whether kids follow *them* or not. We need ministry leaders who will, for the glory of God, lead kids to connect to Jesus daily, weekly, monthly, and yearly.

Simple right?

Not quite. We tend to over-complicate this. I have been guilty for years of over-complicating ministry. I have implemented too many programs, calendared too many events, and over-complicated too many areas in my life. As a result, my spiritual health and my family suffered. Why do we do this? We want to please everyone, so we try and do everything. Someone likes a certain event, even though it wasn't very effective, so we keep doing it...to please people. A church member suggests a certain program and, even though it doesn't fully line up with our vision, we do it anyway...to please people. Maybe we keep some programs around, even though they are past their prime, because if we canceled the program it would make a few people mad. We keep doing what we've always been doing. Why? To please PEOPLE.

The problem is we are trying to please the wrong person. And, because of that, we over complicate the ministry. Maybe we have jealousy towards the church down the street and we want to out-do them. This often means we add more programs. Or we implement the exact same programs that particular church is doing to try and mimic their success. We very rarely cancel programs. We just keep doing them, while adding new programs to the mix. Then we wonder why we are tired and ineffective. It is because we are competing against ourselves. We are not laser-focused in our purpose and pursuits. We become a Jack-of-all-trades and master of none.

Some of us struggle with a Messiah complex, in which we feel like the weight of everyone's spiritual growth rests on our shoulders. We think we are doing Jesus a favor by giving him some time off. For some reason, we think if we weren't in the picture, then nobody would grow spiritually. We like being needed and, because of that, we over-complicate the ministry. What if we could simplify ministry so it was easy to understand? Then it would be more enjoyable and healthier for the church we serve, as well as our family. Let's strip Christianity down to the bare bones and see that our job is simply to help kids connect to Jesus.

Our one purpose, then, is to help kids connect to Jesus daily, weekly, monthly, and yearly. This is what I call the Connect Four strategy. (See Appendix for extended explanation)

Make It Stick

Connect to Jesus. Three words. Simple. Easy to remember. It is incomplete, but it is clear and concise. In his book, *Making Vision Stick*, Andy Stanley writes that for a vision statement to stick, it must first stick in the minds of the people in your ministry. People don't remember or embrace paragraphs; they remember and embrace sentences.

> *"It is better to have a vision statement that is incomplete and memorable than to have one that is complete and forgettable."[4]*

Our purpose statement does not have to communicate the *how*, but it must communicate the *why*. At this point in our journey, we are more concerned with *why* we do what we do, not *how* we do it. We will focus on the *how* later.

What if "helping kids connect to Jesus" was the standard of all we did? What if we calendared *towards* and budgeted *for* helping kids to connect to Jesus daily, weekly, monthly, and yearly? Wouldn't that help us be more laser-focused on the goal? Wouldn't that help us know what to spend our time and resources on?

*It would help us say no to the good things in order to
say yes to the best things.*

The next time we met with our parent council or planning teams to
calendar or budget for the coming year we would have a litmus test
we could compare all programs and events to in order to know
whether we should do them or not. Even good things can hinder
progress when they compete with the best things.

Let this simple, biblical phrase be our bottom line for ministry. It is
the measuring stick of success. It defines the "win" in our ministries.
What is more important than helping kids connect to Jesus? Wasn't
this the ultimate goal Jesus had in mind when he gave His disciples
the Great Commission?

(Recap Reading Experience)

Life is hard. People are broken. Ministry is an attempt to help broken
people become whole and whole people to become broken for broken
people. Pastors are broken too. We over-complicate ministry because
we want to please people. Because of this, we add more programs.
But as we strip ministry down, we see that it is fairly simple.
Ultimately, we have one purpose: to help kids connect to Jesus daily,
weekly, monthly, and yearly. This purpose is simple, direct, and
incomplete. It is not *how* we do what we do, but *why* we do what we
do. It should help keep us focused as we calendar, budget, and
execute the ministries God has entrusted to our care. It also implies
that there will be more than one person connecting to Jesus.

TWO GROUPS
CHAPTER 2

Community Requires Being Together

In the previous chapter we saw the purpose behind everything we do: helping kids connect to Jesus *daily, weekly, monthly, and yearly.* Connecting to Jesus also means connecting to his Body. God calls us to Community. Community means we have to be together. In these next few chapters, we will discover the two most effective ways to encourage togetherness: big group and small group experiences.

What Kids Need

There is an epidemic among young people today called loneliness. It is the fear of never being loved, accepted for who you are, or finding companionship with another person. *Do people actually care about me? Would anyone even notice if I were to leave this earth?* Kids and adults both struggle with the fear of never finding the answer to the burning question, "Where do I belong?" The church should be a place where people find true love, acceptance, and a sense of belonging. But too many people find the exact opposite in church and instead turn to worldly groups to find this type of fellowship.

The following story is a paraphrased excerpt from the book, *"Blue Like Jazz"* by Donald Miller. In his chapter on being alone, he uses this story as a great picture of what so many people experience on a daily basis. Miller writes,

> *"An astronaut is wearing a suit that keeps him alive by recycling his fluids. The astronaut is working on a space station when an accident takes place, and he is cast into*

space to orbit the earth...he is completely alone, without others and without God. He looks out of his bubble helmet at blue earth, reaching toward it, wondering if his friends were still there. He would call to them, but the sound would only come back loud within his helmet. Throughout time his hair would grow long in his helmet and gather around his forehead and across his eyes. Because of this he would not be able to touch his face with his hands to move his hair out of his eyes, so his view of earth slowly, over two years, would dim to only a thin light through a curtain of thatch and beard.

A time came when he couldn't tell whether he was awake or asleep. His thoughts mingled together because he had no person to remind him what was real and what was not. He punched himself in the side to feel pain, and this way he could be sure he was not dreaming. Within ten years he was beginning to breathe heavy through his hair and beard as they were pressing against his face, beginning to curl into his mouth and up his nose. He forgot that he was human. He did not know whether he was a ghost, an apparition, or a demon thing."[5]

The haunting truth of this story is that many kids are just like this floating astronaut, wasting away because of the lack of life being breathed into their souls. They do not always know what they need. Without realizing it, most kids are missing fellowship and community. We were created in the image of a Triune God, meaning that God has fellowship within the Godhead. And since we were created in the image of God we will always have a burning desire to have community and fellowship. Many people will find this need met in worldly groups where God is neither discussed nor welcomed.

All the while, churches are continually requiring their members to put on masks in order to fit into the "club." Sadly, people often find it easier to be authentic *OUTSIDE* the church rather than inside. The most powerful ministry we can have is one where kids are allowed, and even encouraged, to wrestle with real-life issues in the safe and loving community called church. The church, not the world, should be the place where answers to life's toughest questions are found. So, let's give our kids community in our big group and small group experiences.

Together Means Community

Community is a very common theme throughout the Bible. The best example I know is found in Acts 2. The disciples had just experienced the baptism of the Holy Spirit and Peter preached the famous first Christian sermon. Three thousand people became followers of Jesus, and Luke described what these new converts did with their time:

> "They devoted themselves to the apostles' teaching and to fellowship, to the breaking of bread and to prayer. Everyone was filled with awe at the many wonders and signs performed by the apostles. All the believers were *together* and had everything in common. They sold property and possessions to give to anyone who had need. Every day they continued to meet *together in the temple courts.* (Big Group) They *broke bread in their homes* (Small Group) and ate *together* with glad and sincere hearts, *praising God and enjoying the favor of all the people.* And the Lord added to their number daily those who were being saved." ~ *Acts 2:42-47 (NIV) (Emphasis added)*

The early Christians were accustomed to meeting in big group settings at the Temple courts. They were also accustomed to meeting in homes for more intimate, small group times with friends and family. The interesting thing about big and small group settings is that most kids in our ministry already experience these types of groups. In life, big and small group experiences are naturally going to happen. Kids are part of big groups--sporting events, movies, pep rallies, school dances, etc. They also experience small groups during classroom times at school, hanging out with core friends, class projects, teams they play on, etc. They are comfortable in these settings. Let's stop pushing against what is natural and, instead, cultivate what naturally happens to our advantage.

Common Vocabulary

Think about this: What if every leader in our ministries knew exactly what we were trying to accomplish? Wouldn't it make connecting with kids and parents easier? Having a similar vocabulary among our team is crucial for having a common vision. For everyone to know where we are going, we need unity concerning the final destination. But if we are going to help kids connect to Jesus through his people we have to give them opportunities to be *together*.

What if the next time a parent asked us to tell them what our ministry is all about, we could simply say, "We have one purpose: Helping kids connect to Jesus. We do this through two weekly groups: big group and small group experiences. These experiences meet on Sundays at 9am and Wednesdays at 6pm. You should bring your son/daughter and check us out sometime."

Obviously, the times may be different for each church, but the point is clear. One purpose. Two groups. And then we would tell them when and where these experiences meet each week. Wouldn't that simplify communications and be less confusing for people?

Think about it. If we could focus strategically on two major weekly gatherings, big group and small groups, don't you think we would be more effective with the little bit of time we have with our kids? It doesn't matter when our church chooses to have these gatherings. Times and locations are flexible. It's not *when* and *where* that are most important, but *what* and *why*. Each gathering has a specific purpose. We don't want to do the same thing during big group time as we do in small groups, but we do want to be intentional with the influential time we have with them.

For most churches, big group time will be the gateway, or entry point, for new kids to enter our ministries. This does not mean big group is more important than small group. I personally think small groups have more potential for spiritual growth and formation. Because of this, I believe that small groups should be open groups, where anyone can join at any time. This doesn't necessarily mean they will be the entry point for new kids to join. It just means kids can get involved in a small group at any time throughout the year. Small group gatherings are not the entry point for most churches.

> *[Note: there may also be a need for closed groups designed for deeper discipleship purposes. But, we will discuss small groups in more detail in chapter four.]*

I usually see churches become more successful in reaching new kids with the big group gatherings. Unless they are designed with lost kids in mind, small groups are too revealing and intimate for the average person. It takes some time to feel comfortable enough with our ministry before they will move to a small group setting.

Before you object to what I've just shared, look at your church. Not just your youth or children's ministry, your whole church. I have never been to a church that had more people in small groups than they did in big church. I know there are churches in the world that have more people in small groups than big groups. However, these churches are called underground churches, and they would be persecuted greatly if they met in large numbers in public.

America is a culture of people that "window shop" before they buy anything. Chances are, most of the people who visit our churches have already peeped through our blinds, looking at our websites, just to see if we are what they want. We don't have to agree that this is good. But we do need to acknowledge that it is happening, and we should be prepared to respond to the culture in relevant ways.

If we don't, then we are telling the lost world that they are not as important as we say they are.

Plan to Win

I once heard a story of a man walking through the woods, where he noticed one tree after another with targets drawn on them. Each target had an arrow stuck into it. The amazing thing was not the targets, but the arrows. Whoever had done this must have been a master archer.

Every shot was right in the middle of the bull's-eye. The man explored the area more, until he finally came across a mysterious figure of a Robin Hood-type person.

The explorer asked the man, "Did you hit all those bull's-eyes?"

"I sure did!" declared the archer.

"Wow! That's AMAZING! Can you show me how to do that?" asked the man.

The archer smiled and said, "It's easy! Watch and learn."

The archer lifted his bow and arrow. The onlooker was trembling with excitement to watch such a skilled guru aim and release the stunningly crafted arrow into the air towards another tree. The man shot. The arrow hit. The archer walked up to the tree, pulled out a paintbrush, and proceeded to draw a target around the arrow. "Bull's eye again!" proclaimed the archer. Of course, the explorer was thoroughly disappointed.

I share this to illustrate how most churches do ministry. Ministry leaders can sometimes resemble the archer in this story. If we aren't careful, we will do ministry with no strategy and then celebrate the results as if we planned it that way. The truth is, many times we *stumble* upon success simply because God is gracious and we preached the Bible. God's word will always do what it was sent out to accomplish. Still, the results could have been much better if only we had planned properly. So let's plan. The next two chapters will give us a strategy for making the most out of our big group and small group times. But before we move on, we need to define the "win" for each group.

Defining the "Win"

The "win" for our big group time is not *entertainment*. The "win" is *experience*. Entertainment may or may not happen at our big group gatherings, but that's not the main thing. We are trying to help kids have a positive and meaningful *experience* where they feel welcomed and accepted just the way they are. We want kids to experience the presence of Christ in our environments, our presentations, and the content we share.

The "win" for our small group time is not education. The "win" is relationship. Education will only happen when kids know they are loved and accepted. The saying is true, "People don't care how much you know until they know how much you care." We want every student to have meaningful heart connections with loving, Christian adults and teens that will lead them to the throne of grace every week. Of course, there should be a teaching planner we follow in order to ensure education.

However, too many ministry leaders neglect the *method* for the sake of the *message*. This makes it hard for the kids to digest the *message*. Education will happen. Trust me. But education should always be secondary to relationships. Always. So, let's look at how to make the *message* palatable for those we aim to educate.

(Recap Reading Experience)

Community is a biblical theme. Our environment should be set up in a way that makes it easy for kids to have community. Kids have to be together in order to have community. Kids thrive when they hang out in big group *and* small group settings. Big group will probably be the most effective gathering for inviting unchurched kids into the ministry. The goal of big group is to move kids to a small group. The "win" for big group is not entertainment, but experience. The "win" for small group is not education, but relationship. *Education happens with the messages we teach in big group and small group settings.*

BIG GROUP
CHAPTER 3

Community Requires Being Together in Big Groups

Before we get started with these next two chapters, remember this: nothing trumps the favor of God on our ministries. So as we talk about details, which could enhance our big group and small group experiences, please don't neglect seeking the favor of the Lord.

There are few men who have impacted my life more than Dave Busby. I never met the man before he passed, and it wasn't until the past few years that I was even introduced to his books or teachings. Yet, his ministry has profoundly impacted many of the spiritual giants who have had a lasting impact on my life. So, the domino effect happened: my life was changed through their lives being changed. Now, as I read his book, *The Heart of the Matter*, I am personally impacted by his words. Busby shares the following story to open his book,

> *"There I am, the sun beating down on my head, sweat running down my face. I'm in the middle of the desert desperately trying to quench my thirst. With my bare hands, I'm clawing through the sand, digging hole after miserable hole. I'm trying to find water to satisfy me, to put out the fire that burns deep inside of me. As I look around, I see hundreds of my failed attempts to dig a well. I'm exhausted. I'm frustrated. I want to give up. But I can't stop. I must keep digging and digging, searching and searching. I'm convinced my hard work will eventually pay off and my thirst will be quenched. If only I would stand still for a moment and rest, I would see the well already there in front of me, waiting for me to drink."*[6]

What a powerful picture of how we do ministry. We work so hard to make sure all the details are right and our presentation is attractive, and we often neglect drinking from the well. I have been in churches that had everything going for them. They had the best lights, the highest quality sound system, the nicest building, and the best ministry tools the church could offer. Yet the spirit in the room was that of spiritual apathy. However, I have also been in old, smelly rooms with a handful of kids who had no special lighting, no stage, a static-prone sound system, and no ministry tools. But they were drinking from the well, and the Spirit of God was all over their ministry.

The pages to follow include lots of great ideas for strengthening your big group and small group experiences. Yes, we should care about putting on the best quality program we can. But don't rely on these pages to guarantee your ministry will be fruitful. Instead, focus on this principle:

Leading kids to drink from the well is much more important than getting every detail right.

Big Group Experiences

We just learned in our previous chapter that the "win" for our big group gathering is not entertainment, but experience. It is our job to set up our big group times with this priority in mind. In keeping with the big group experiences our kids are already a part of, our big group times should be fun and energetic. Also, big group times should be well staffed with capable volunteers who will champion a welcoming spirit and foster healthy relationships with every student who walks through the doors. (See chapter six on volunteers) Andy Stanley shares in his book, *Deep and Wide*, that North Point church evaluates every program by asking three questions. We will spend the remainder of this chapter discussing each question together:

1. Is the environment appealing?
2. Is the presentation engaging?
3. Is the content helpful?[7]

Evaluating Our Environment

The environment for our big group gatherings should be appealing to kids. If they wouldn't hang out in your ministry area on Friday night don't expect them to be excited about hanging out on Wednesday or Sunday. I'm not saying we should open our doors every Friday night. I'm simply saying that we need to start looking at the venues in which our kids are naturally spending time in and try to mimic those settings as much, and as appropriately, as possible.

Starbucks, for instance, has calm lighting and comfortable seating areas to encourage conversations. Malls play music quietly in the background to help set the mood. Movie theaters usually have a small place to play, eat, and mingle until the movie doors open, and videos and announcements rolling on the screen until the movie begins. The sound systems in these venues are not cracking or popping. The area is never dirty or smelly. The lighting is always perfect for the setting we find ourselves in. These strategies are intentional. They are setting us up to have a positive and unique experience. There is a reason kids like Starbucks or the mall. The setting is appealing. I know we don't have the budget these businesses have, but that doesn't give us the right to let our areas go uncleaned and look boring. Have you ever heard of Pinterest? Think creative, not expensive.

Why not ask our kids or teenagers to help us remodel our rooms? They know what they like better than we do, anyway. Give them a dollar amount and tell them to get going. It may surprise you what they can do if given a bit of guidance and the opportunity. Plus, they are more likely to invite their friends to a room they designed than a room we designed.

There should always be age appropriate, kid-friendly music playing before they arrive. No organ music allowed. Preschool and children ministry leaders, play the latest VBS songs. MS and HS leaders, play whatever Christian artists your teens are into at the time. There should be places for kids to sit, play, talk, and eat. Oh yeah! And if the budget allows, there should be food too. This could be something as cheap as popcorn, nachos, chips and dip, or something.

Better yet, have your church members sign up to take turns bringing food. The adults in your church might fall in love with students by simply cooking them a meal. Kids love to eat and they congregate around the food bar. Conversations naturally happen around a meal, whether steak and potato or just chips and dips.

Remember that we are trying to set the mood for relationships to be built.

No matter what we do, we must keep our areas looking and smelling clean, void of any boring or blank walls, and stocked with *UP-TO-DATE* material. No out-of-date event posters. Kids don't like out of date milk, so why would we leave old flyers on our walls?

By the way, maybe your budget doesn't allow for event posters. However, certain events might send posters to you for free if you ask. And you could invest in cheap poster boards and different colored markers from a hobby store and let your kids create informational posters for your ministry. This would help get the word out for your events, and you would be encouraging kids to serve by using their gifts and talents for Christ.

Evaluating Our Presentation

The presentation for our big groups should be engaging to kids. We should be intentional about sharing the Gospel in every message. No matter what topic we teach, we should always land the plane facing the cross and explain how our relationship with Jesus is the ultimate answer to life's questions. Our teaching should not be boring. I know. I know. When a person offers me a stick of gum I usually think to myself, "Are they saying my breath stinks?" No, I'm not saying you are the worst teacher in the history of the church. All I'm saying is we need to make sure we give the weekly lesson as much attention as we give Netflix. After all, this is the message that transforms lives. We have been given the ministry of reconciliation, as though God were making His appeal through us! (2 Corinthians 5:18-20)

I do know one thing. I know that I am not the best preacher on the face of this earth. I'm not even close. But I am a million times better than I was when I preached my first sermon. I remember having the opportunity to preach one Sunday night at my church. I had prepared all week for this moment. I was confident that I understood the passage I was to preach and I knew what my main point was. That night, I preached the entire chapter of John 21. I thought surely a whole chapter would take more time than I had available to me. I got up; I preached; I sat down. TEN MINUTES! I don't know how I preached John 21 in ten minutes...oh wait...of course I do...I didn't know what I was doing. I even mispronounced Nathanael's name.

A short while afterwards I had the opportunity to preach at a church down the road, again on a Sunday night. I was halfway through my sermon when I completely drew a blank. I had no idea where I was going with an illustration I was sharing. And of course I didn't carry notes with me back then. Suddenly, an elderly woman in the crowd yelled from the back of the worship center, "Maybe we better pray!" I never felt so embarrassed in my life. I was so bad at preaching that the people were begging for prayer. Well, I guess that's not all that bad...

You see, I am an introvert by nature and when God called me to preach, I freaked out. I knew who I was, and preaching was not it. I ran from God for several years before I finally surrendered to his calling on my life. And then it took years for me to get any good at preaching. Many times I told God, "See God! I told you I wasn't any good at this stuff." But God would gently remind me that it's not my problem. It's His. I knew what God had called me to, so I pressed on.

My point in sharing this is to encourage you to never stop practicing your presentation skills. We have the most important message in the world. We have been given stewardship of this message, and how we present it matters. To this day, I will pray about the message I am about to preach. I will preach it to myself all week. And then I will record myself preaching it so I can hear any articulation flaws I might have. Why do I do this? Because I know Preston Cave and he is not a natural born preacher. But I know the Preston Cave God has called me to be, and the message He has entrusted me to preach. I take that very seriously.

So first, I spend time making the passage I'm about to preach personal to me. Then I spend the rest of my time making it engaging for the audience I'm about to preach to. God will empower us to do what he has called us to do. But He also expects us to work at it. Our presentations for our big group times should engage our audience in the story of God redeeming them back to Himself.

Evaluating Our Content

The content we share for our big group times should be helpful. And it should always be biblical. I have heard many preachers pray, "Lord, anoint my words today." I would always think to myself, "God has already anointed *HIS* words. If we want to *be* anointed then we need to *preach* the anointed." It's that simple. Does this mean we should only teach verse-by-verse lessons? Not necessarily. Remember the audience we serve. Topical teaching is just as important as verse-by-verse teaching. Why? Because kids have questions and we have answers. We should have a yearly calendar with plans to teach on relevant topics on certain days of the year. For teenagers, dating is a great topic to teach during the month of February. "New beginnings", "Reset", or "Do-Over" are great lesson titles during the beginning of school or New Years. Teach on Christmas during Christmas. And please don't teach a children's lesson to high school teens, or a teen message to first grade kids. Know your audience and teach age-specific material. Follow the life of your kids and "as we are going, make disciples." (Matthew 28)

I have heard people criticize topical teaching as if it were from the devil. And then they would teach a whole series on soteriology. That's topical too. I have nothing against topical teaching, provided we use proper exegesis and hermeneutics with every passage. Heck, even Jesus taught topically from time to time...actually ALL the time! Remember when Jesus taught in parables? Or when he would use the environment around him to make a point? The fig tree? The field that was white for harvest? The coin in the fish's mouth? I could go on. But the point is clear. Jesus actually taught more topically than any other method.

One could argue that he might have taught verse-by-verse when he read from the scroll in Luke 4, but all we see here is him reading two verses. This cannot be considered verse-by-verse teaching. Interestingly enough, verse numbers didn't even exist in the Bible until the 1550's. So for the first 1,500 years of Christianity there was no such thing as "verse-by-verse" teaching. Remember that the next time someone condemns you for topical teaching.

A Case FOR Verse-by-Verse Teaching

I don't mean to sound like I'm against verse-by-verse teaching. I actually love it. But I don't think it should be the only, or even primary, method of teaching for our family ministries. Jesus taught topically most of the time, yet Jesus was the Word made flesh. So, every time he opened his mouth he was also, in a real sense, teaching verse-by-verse. He always had a high view of the Old Testament scriptures. Haddon Robinson says,

> *"Expository teaching, at its core, is more a philosophy than a method. Whether a man can be called an expositor starts with his purpose and with his honest answer to the question, 'Do you, as a teacher, endeavor to bend your thought to scripture, or do you use scripture to support your thought?'* "[8]

That is why, many years ago, I adapted the "Rifleman's Creed" from the movie "Full Metal Jacket." I mixed it with a few other churches' Bible commitments. Every week, I have my kids repeat this commitment out loud after me. They like it very much. Here is my "Bible Creed":

> *This is my Bible. There are many like it, but this one is mine. I will read it. I will study it. I will live it out. I will not let my opinions tell me what my Bible means. Instead, I will let my Bible tell me what my opinions should be.*

However we choose to teach or preach, make sure the content is helpful to the hearer. What's the purpose of knowledge that doesn't transform? Education is not the win in preaching. Transformation is the win. Education will happen, but transformation is the goal. Whatever we preach or teach let the content be helpful.

Big Groups Are Essential

When comedians or other performers speak to kids they will often want the lights in the room to be dim. Why? If the lights are too bright the kids may not laugh. Kids and teenagers are afraid of laughing at the wrong time and embarrassing themselves. But if the lights are dimmed, they can take off their masks for a moment and hide in the darkness.

This truth is why big group settings are so important. Sometimes we just need to let kids hide in the crowd until they are ready to go deeper. This is also why big group should be designed with guests in mind. We are much more likely to have first-time guests come to our big group gatherings rather than to our small groups. Small groups are often too intimate for a first-time guest. However, kids are willing to hide in a crowd and watch from a distance to see if our message is right for them. Small groups are the second step, not the first. (see preface to understand how I used these principles in smaller churches) Sure, there are a few kids who freak out in large crowds and would much rather be with only a few close friends. For these kids, let our small group ministry be their *first* step. Don't require kids to attend big group first before getting involved in a small group. Each student is different.

Still, the majority of kids prefer big group to small group as the entry point into our ministry. Most kids want to follow from a distance before diving head first into Christianity. There's a reason some churches are moving towards an online campus experience. Some people want to peep through our window to see if we are real and sincere. If they trust us, they will come hangout with us.

Before you judge them, remember that Nicodemus wasn't willing to meet Jesus in broad daylight the first time he encountered him. Nicodemus was curious, and if hiding in the dark was what it would take for him to eventually become a follower then Jesus was willing to meet him in the darkness. Remember, too, that all the disciples followed Jesus at a distance after his arrest. Sometimes kids need the same thing. They need a safe place to "come and see" before they can go all-in with this Jesus thing. Give them a place to hide in a big group setting, and we will see more kids come to Christ. Then we can move them to a small group.

(Recap Reading Experience)

Big group experiences are important. They should be fun, energetic, and welcoming. They will most likely be the entry point for most kids. We evaluate our big group gathering by asking three questions: (1) Is the environment appealing? (2) Is the presentation engaging? (3) Is the content helpful? Big group is where kids can hide so they can "come and see" before they get involved in a small group. The ultimate goal of our big group is to invite guests to embrace the gospel and to move them towards a small group.

SMALL GROUPS
CHAPTER 4

Community Requires being Together in Small Groups

Few ministries have more potential for impacting a life than small groups. For better or for worse, kids are actively involved in these types of groups throughout their elementary, middle, and high school tenure. I hope you will allow me to be transparent for a moment. If not, then skip the following story:

> *I was seventeen when I first became introduced to the magic and impact of a small group. It was just me and a few of my close friends. We would meet on a regular basis for fun and fellowship. We often connected with each other throughout the week. We liked the same music, were about the same age, and spent hours each week talking about life and our future in a circle of trust, love, and acceptance....OH YEAH...and listening to Metallica around a water bong. (Hear me out)*
>
> *I was ten when I gave my life to the Lord at a preteen camp in Clayton, OK. I was fifteen when I first felt the call to ministry. But that was also the time when I began to rebel. I was scared to death that God might want me to be in ministry, not because I had this grand vision of being rich and famous, but because I was an extreme introvert. I was terrified of talking to groups of people. So I ran from the call.*
>
> *When I was seventeen I got involved with a small group of guys who were pretty cool—and they accepted me in their circle. I was with them until I graduated high school. Shortly after graduation, I had a horrible car accident that God used to wake me up to my lifestyle and to draw me back to him. That is a different, and truly miraculous story. But the point is, I was a huge hypocrite my last two years of high school.*

There were many times I would be sitting with those guys smoking weed, and the Holy Spirit would whisper to my heart, "Preston, this is not you. Why are you doing this?"

Now, here is where it gets interesting. I often look back on those times and a small part of me really misses that small group. Not because I desire to relive that lifestyle or I miss the feelings of separation from the Lord during that season of life, but because it was the first time I truly felt fellowship in a close way with other people. The sad thing is it took a few years for me to find that same sense of closeness in the church. Yet, the church is the only place where real life can be found, so it is important for us to get this thing right. Why? If we don't get this right, our kids will find community in small groups outside the church where the true source of life is often not welcomed. Let's help students find Jesus in the community of a small group.

Small Group Experiences

So, what does a small group look like? There are many books on this subject. Just remember that this book is only giving a skeleton of family ministry. It is your job, as the ministry leader, to choose the meat you want on the bones. But I will tell you what we do, and then we will talk about it. However, first, let's define "small group." A small group is a group of two or more kids with a leader. Depending on the size of your church, you might have a small group with two kids or a small group with twenty kids. The ideal size, to me, is between eight to fifteen kids.

We believe kids don't care what we know until they know that we care. We believe in open groups that are welcoming to all kinds of people. Now, I know there is a time for deeper discipleship. And there may be times to have closed groups for accountability purposes. (See www.disciple6.com for info on Discipleship groups) However, Grant Byrd, student pastor of FBC McKinney once said,

> *"Sometimes I have a student tell me that they are not growing in our ministry. I then ask them, 'When was the last time you shared the Gospel with someone?' Every time they admit to never sharing the Gospel. And then I say, 'You might not be growing, but that's not the church's fault. You need to start sharing the gospel, because you can't go any deeper than the gospel.'"*

This is one reason why we keep our groups open. We want non-Christian kids to feel welcome to come and explore the faith. We want to encourage Christian kids to feel they can invite their friends to the groups. We know that the average unchurched child would rather come to the big group time rather than the small group time. But most of those kids won't make decisions at big group. Why? They don't want to stand in front of the big group. They often will be introduced to the gospel and may even secretly give their hearts to Christ while in the big group. But they tend to "come out" as a follower of Jesus in a small group.

What better experience for the group than for an unbeliever to give his or her life to Jesus in front of everyone else? Open groups allow guests, but they also allow hurting Christians to join as well. We believe a healthy mix for a small group is to have some mature

Christian kids, some hurting or doubting Christian kids, and some who are unchurched. Why? If the group is full of Christian kids only, then it can become a holy huddle where no evangelism takes place. They live in a Christian bubble and never live in the real world. If there are only hurting Christians in the group, then it becomes a gripe session. And we could only imagine what conversations there would be if the groups were only unchurched kids. But if there is a healthy balance then each group will have great conversations and unique perspectives.

Andy Stanley once said, *"Circles are better than rows."* Because of this, we encourage kids at our big group meetings to join a small group. And during our small group meetings, we don't meet in classrooms with rows and one teacher with podium up front. We don't do "Sunday School" either. We may meet on Sunday morning at the church, but we don't call it "Sunday School". The reason we don't call it "Sunday School" is because of the word *"school"* and because of the word *"Sunday"*.

Why not "School"?

"School" is the last place a kid wants to be after spending an entire week at school. Also, the term "school" implies education. Don't get me wrong. Education is very important. But if education is the focus, then education will become the "win". Getting through the lesson will be the most important thing about the meeting. Relationships will become secondary. Andy Stanley says in his book, *Deep and Wide,*

> *"Remember, teaching through the entire Bible doesn't create Bible scholars anyway. It creates people who think they are*

Bible scholars. And those are some of the meanest, most uncompassionate humans beings on the planet...Remember the widow who gave everything she had? Jesus liked her more than the Pharisees. She was a doer. Jesus liked doers. I imagine he still does."[9]

If education is the only "win," it can breed snobby, pompous Christians who couldn't care less about the needs of others. Do you want that type of person in your ministry? Me either. Remember:

Education is not the "win." Relationships are the "win." Actually, transformation is the "win" and relationships are often a step towards transformation.

If we can get our small group leaders to build significant heart connections with their kids, then education is a by-product. Think about it. Do you really care what somebody believes if you know they don't care about you and what you believe?

We all have people in our lives that love us unconditionally. I can think of a person now. I respect them, I know they love me, and I want to know what makes that person tick. I want what they have. Remember that with kids, the Bible is more caught than taught. One of our church members, Bob Raus, once sat in my office and reminded me of this truth:

We don't teach the Bible. We teach KIDS the Bible.

Why not "Sunday"?

Sunday implies *Sunday*. I know. I'm a genius, right? Think about it. "Sunday School" could never meet any other day than Sunday. Why? Because of the name. But if we believe kids would benefit spiritually from being connected to a small group, why wouldn't we choose the best day for more kids to get involved in a small group? What if some kids can't meet on Sunday, but they could on Monday? Or Tuesday? Or Wednesday? You get the picture. Let's remove any barriers the church has unintentionally put up, in order to help more kids connect to Jesus together through small groups.

At my church our preschool, children, and middle school students still meet on Sundays for small groups. However, our high school small groups meet on Wednesday nights after the big group time and the sermon. We accomplish both big group and small group on the same night. There are more high school kids during this time, and high school teens are becoming more and more busy every year. Plus, studies are showing that, anatomically speaking, a high school student has trouble falling asleep before 11pm. This means that high school teens are more alert in the evening than they are in the morning. If they are more capable of learning in the evening then why wouldn't we allow them to have small groups at night?

Also, this frees up Sunday to allow high school students to serve. We will talk more about this in chapter five. But this would never be possible if these groups were called "Sunday School" classes. See my point? They are still getting a small group experience. It just so happens that it's not on a Sunday.

Note: It is important to have the support from your family ministry team as well as your executive leadership BEFORE trying to make a change like this. In order for this shift to work it has to be a team effort. This is not a necessary component to a healthy ministry. It is just something my church does that I really think is more efficient than other models. However, if your church is not ready for a shift like this then don't force it. This will not make or break your family ministry model.

What Kids Need Most

In his book, *Creating a Lead Small Culture*, Reggie Joiner talks about what kids need in order to anchor their lives to something solid. He says kids need nouns. Nouns are clear, tangible, and concrete.[10]

So, what are the nouns Joiner is talking about? By definition, a noun is a person, a place, a thing, or an idea. Joiner encourages his readers to give every student a *person* who believes in them and a safe *place* to belong. I agree with his exhortation, but I would go a step further and say there is more to a noun than that. What about the *thing*? The *idea*? Kids need those, too. So yes, every student needs nouns in their lives. They need a *person* who loves them: before they can believe in God, they need a person who believes in them. They need a *place* to belong. They also need a *thing* to believe in. And they need an *idea* to live for. So, let's see how we can use nouns in our small group ministry to accomplish our purpose.

Give Kids a Person

The following material is applicable to kids of all ages. If we give preschool and children's ministry kids this type of person then it is preventative medicine for the MS and HS ministries. Remember that we are all in this together. Kids need a person to believe in them before they can believe in themselves and believe in God. Actually, kids need more than one person. Studies have shown that kids are much more likely to stay connected to a church after graduation if they have significant heart connections with multiple Christian adults.

Dr. Richard Ross is a student ministry professor at Southwestern Baptist Theological Seminary in Fort Worth, TX. He has written a book I highly recommend, *Student Ministry and the Supremacy of Christ*. Ross explains that in the 1940's and 1950's, Christians started to realize this new adolescent culture emerging. The rise of the youth culture was also a rise in Para church organizations, with guys like Jim Rayburn starting Young Life, Torrey Johnson with Youth for Christ, Bill Bright and Campus Crusade for Christ, and many others. Ross says,

> "*Early Para church leaders tended to be younger, creative, and relational. They were just right as missionaries to an unreached people group.*(See Appendix 3) *Many of those Para church ministries experienced visible success that caught the attention of church leaders...soon most congregations were looking for someone young, creative, and relational around whom teenagers would flock.*"[11]

This gave way to churches beginning to separate kids from the rest of the church altogether. That is never healthy. Mark Oestreicher says,

> "Isolated age groups have done just as much harm as good. Isolation might make things easier in some ways, but striving for the best is rarely easy."[12]

Kids are not just the future of the church. They are the present church of today as well. The Para church movement also led to the model of ministry many churches still use to this day. This model says that the discipleship of the child/teenager and the numerical growth of the ministry fall on the shoulders of the ministry leaders. Churches adopted the Para church model, designed primarily for ministering to *non-Christians*, and churches have wondered why they only develop shallow Christian children and teens, many of which walk away from the faith after the thrills are gone. There is a better way.

Ross reminds his readers that scripture is clear that the father and mother are to be the primary spiritual leaders to kids. He would then quote Merton Strommen and Richard Hardel's book, *Passing on the Faith: A Radical New Model for Youth and Family Ministry,*

> "Research suggests teenagers also need a minimum of three adults outside the home to prosper emotionally and spiritually." [13]

Oestreicher agrees with this statement when he says, *"teenagers need adults in their lives - multiple adults."* [14]

Reggie Joiner makes a great observation by saying,

> "*Think about it. If you are reading this right now, chances are you believe what you believe and you do what you do because of the way someone influenced your life. More than likely, it wasn't just one person, but several.*"[15]

So, it's clear that kids need multiple adults in their lives in order to thrive. It is our job, as leaders, to create environments where these relationships are encouraged and nurtured. We need leaders who will show kids what God looks like. Joiner says,

> "*People can't see God. People can't see Jesus. People can't see the Holy Spirit. But people can see people who follow God. People can see the church.*"[16]

In his book, Richard Ross gives his readers the foundational principles for ministry, which are listed below:

1.   Ministry begins with a focus on the supremacy of Christ.
2.   Kids are most likely to embrace the full supremacy of Christ when they have heart connections with significant adults in their lives who increasingly embrace the full supremacy of Christ.
3.   The highest priority in ministry is leading parents and other adults who are significant to kids increasingly to embrace the full supremacy of Christ.
4.   The second highest priority in ministry is leading kids and the significant adults in their lives to build heart connections with each other - and then to live out the full supremacy of Christ *together*. (Emphasis added)

5. The third highest priority in ministry is designing programming that allows kids to build heart connections with peers and to live out the full supremacy of Christ *together*. (Emphasis mine)[17]

In other words, we should be running hard and fast after Jesus. We should then look around us and see which adults are keeping up. We should ask those adults to pour into the lives of our kids. Then we should resource them to coach their kids to run hard and fast after Jesus, so they start to pursue God *together*. Joiner makes this point:

> *"Although the average church can never compete with what culture can produce, culture can never compete with what the average church can do in the life of a kid."*[18]

So, what do we ask from our small group leaders? Again, Joiner has the answer. Here are five principles for every small group leader. To see the explanations of these principles, download the Lead Small app.

- Be Present
    - Show up predictably
    - Show up mentally
    - Show up randomly
- Create a Safe Place
    - Lead the group
    - Respect the process
    - Guard the heart

- Partner with Parents
  - Cue the parent
  - Honor the parent
  - Reinforce the family
- Make it Personal
  - Live in community
  - Set priorities
  - Be real
- Move them Out
  - Move them to someone else
  - Move them to be the church
  - Move them to what's next

Let's give kids a person and a place...

Give Kids a Place

Every child needs a place to belong. This is important because when a kid moves from children's ministry and enters middle school they will need to have that safe place to belong in order to help them navigate adolescence. If they experienced this type of safe place in preschool and children's ministry they will be much more likely to embrace it in MS and HS. Mark Oestreicher shares that the purpose of adolescence is to help kids with identity, autonomy, and affinity. In other words, adolescence is a time when teenagers answer the questions: Who am I? What am I good at? Where do I belong?

Identity is answering the question, "Who am I?" Kids walk around every day putting on masks for every group they are part of.

They have a church mask, a circle of friends mask, a boyfriend/girlfriend mask, a mask for their parents, as well as many other masks they wear each day in order to fit in. Exhausting, right? Well, let's give them a safe place to belong. Let's give them a place they can take off the masks and be who they were made to be. If they don't learn to take off the masks, one day they are going to look in the mirror and forget what is reality and what is just another mask. They will look at their reflection and ask, "Who is this person staring back at me?" Why not let our small groups be the one place where they can really be themselves? Wouldn't that be refreshing? Small groups could help answer the question, "Who am I?"

If fact, small groups could help kids answer the other two questions of adolescence as well. "What am I good at?" is the next one. Small groups are the best avenues for service projects and other activities that could help kids answer this question. And small groups, if they are allowed to be organic, meaning that they form and grow through natural relationships, can become the affinity groups for our kids. They learn that they can belong in this safe place called small groups.

The idea of giving kids a place also means there has to be an actual physical location the group meets each week. It was many years ago when I led a small group at a Super Summer Evangelism Training camp for one week. We were going to be meeting in the same place several times per day, all five days, for small group interactions. In the very first gathering I told the group that the tree we were sitting under was going to be our "holy ground". We would meet here, in the same spot, all week long. We were going to love on each other and encourage one another to grow closer to the Lord.

The week was awesome. And the last day I bought a bunch of Ziploc bags and a spoon. I had every student scoop up dirt to put in their bags to take back home with them. I challenged the group to put the dirt in a jar and place it somewhere that they would see it. This became a reminder to us of what God did that week. I still have my jar of dirt sitting on my shelf in the office. This was a physical place we met which became a sacred refuge for our group.

What can we learn from this? If possible, don't move from place to place each week. There is something important about consistency. And there is something about having a physical place to belong. Give kids the best location, so they can have a refuge from their hectic lives, and let's not move from that spot unless we absolutely have to.

[Note: I have been at churches where having a consistent physical space was not realistic. The building was too small for everyone in the church, and every space was a shared space. Jane Wilson, one of my mentors and a discipleship specialist for Texas Baptists, says, "Perhaps it's the corner of a gym in which they can meet. They might not be able to post anything on the walls to make it theirs, but it is still consistent. The physical place is important. But, the emotional safety is even more so."]

Let's give kids a person, a place, and a thing...

Give Kids a Thing

We don't need to rehash what we already talked about in our section in the previous chapter concerning the content we share. But I will reiterate, God's story is the "thing" kids need most. If we aren't giving them the Bible then we are wasting the small amount of time we have with them. Don't waste their time with insignificant information that has no power to transform their lives. We need to be intentional with the information we present. It needs to point to the goal we've decided upon.

Let's give kids a person, a place, a thing, and an idea...

Give Kids an Idea

Kids need to know they are the church *right now*. We need to help them be the church while they are still with us, so that when they leave us they will know how to be the church without us. As kids get into high school, we should give them opportunities to serve and help cultivate within them a vision of how their story can fit into God's bigger story. We believe the best thing we could do for kids, apart from introducing them to Christ, is to help them find the vision God has for their lives.

The more opportunities to serve, the more mission trips, the more camps and leadership conferences we empower kids to attend, the better their chances are of hearing from God as to their life calling.

Every chance we get we should be encouraging kids to pray for God to give them a vision. Why? Simple. Calling matters. Matthew 14:22-31 tells the story of Peter walking on water. I'm sure you know it, so I'm not going to go over the whole story now. I just want to point out a few things. When the disciples saw Jesus, they became afraid. After Jesus introduced himself to them, they still were afraid--all but Peter. Peter looked at Jesus and said, "Lord, if that is you, *tell* me to come to you on the water." Now, why would Peter say that? Why wouldn't he just say, "Lord, *can* I come to you on the water?" Instead, Peter almost commands Jesus to "*tell*" him to come. You know the story. Jesus says, "Come." Peter walks on water. Peter sinks because of doubt. Jesus saves him. They climb back in the boat, while the other disciples watch in amazement.

But let's get back to the way Peter talked to Jesus. I believe Peter understood something we sometimes forget. I think Peter knew that if he could just get Jesus to *tell* him to walk on water, then Peter would actually be able to do it. And that leads to this principle:

What God calls us to do He empowers us to do.

We should help kids find their life calling so they will have confidence in what God wants from them. What God call our kids to do, He will empower our kids to do. And they need to know that. I truly believe that if we could help kids grab a big idea from the Lord they would jump out of the boat as fast as Peter did. And they could turn the world upside down!

(Recap Reading Experience)

Small group experiences are important. Our small group experience should give kids nouns. Nouns are a person, a place, a thing, and an idea. The *person* is the small group leader. Small group leaders should be present, create a safe place, partner with parents, make it personal, and move them out. The *place* should be safe and should be a physical, unchanging location. The *thing* is God's story throughout history. The *idea* is the calling kids should have from God on how their story fits into his story. It is our job to give kids a person, a place, a thing, and an idea.

THREE DECISIONS
CHAPTER 5

Spiritual Formation Made Easy

I want to spend a moment reminding us that this model of ministry is our skeleton, not the comprehensive expression of *all* we do in our ministry. When I say we should focus more on our two weekly gatherings, I don't mean to say we should *only* focus on these two gatherings. There is a real need for monthly get-togethers, service projects, V.B.S., summer camps, mission trips, conferences, and a place for the more committed kids to go deeper.

But I am convinced that most churches today have no strategy in place for the average child or teenager to connect to Jesus daily, weekly, monthly, and yearly. Most churches today are just going through the motions, doing a model of ministry that worked twenty, or even thirty, years ago--with no real grasp on why they aren't making a significant impact on the community in which they serve.

So, I want to focus on spiritual formation, which can be the standard of ministry for a church of any size. It is simple to understand and applies to any child, regardless of age, who enters our doors. Every person we encounter will fall into one of these three categories. Every kid will either need to meet Jesus for the first time, fall in love with Jesus through discipleship and worship, or serve Jesus in some sort of personal ministry. That's it. This is what I like to call spiritual formation for dummies.

It is our job, as ministry leaders, to help every kid make all three decisions. Our goal should never be to *just* get kids "saved." Jesus didn't die on the cross for us to make converts. He calls us to make disciples. So yes, we should hope that every child, at some point or another, meets Jesus for the first time. But this is not the end; it is only the beginning. After they meet Jesus, we help them fall in love with him through our big group and small group experiences. And as kids fall more deeply in love with him, they will naturally want to serve him. Again, we use our big group and small group experiences for this.

> *Preschool Leaders: You might be wondering how to get your preschool kiddos to serve in ministry, so here are a few ideas to think about. Try getting them to bring toothpaste or a canned food item to help the local food pantry. Encourage them to bring change from their piggy banks to send to a mission's organization. Maybe talk to your pastor about using them in a Sunday service to help sing, partner with the deacons to pass the offering plate, or stand with their parents and greet at the front doors. Be creative with your kiddos and know that whatever you do, whether large or small, is part of the overall family ministry strategy to develop them to move towards maturity.*

Here is the secret to success:

For the discipleship process to have a lasting impact it doesn't start with evangelism, it ends with evangelism.

Evangelism is often the only focus of churches. Don't get me wrong; I love evangelism. I spent several years traveling full-time with a focus in evangelism, helping churches reach their cities through school assemblies and nighttime outreach events. The ministry I served with saw thousands each year give their lives to Jesus. It was amazing. But I noticed something along the way. The churches who were *less* successful in their outreach efforts were the churches with no foundation in place to properly disciple the new converts we were helping them reach. They focused on evangelism FIRST, but Jesus didn't do that.

One of the all-time best books I have ever read is a small book by Dr. Robert Coleman, *The Master Plan of Evangelism.*[19] This is a must-read for any ministry leader wanting to understand the way Jesus did ministry.

In his book, Dr. Coleman suggests that Jesus' strategy for world evangelism was not to have tons of city-wide crusades bringing in the masses with a "wow-factor" event in hopes to get people to pray a prayer. Not that these events are wrong in and of themselves. I have been a part of hundreds of these types of events. But if the event is the only thing the church focuses on, their evangelistic efforts will show little to no lasting fruit. Coleman gives us eight chapters and eight principles on Jesus' evangelism strategy. I will comment on each very briefly, but would highly recommend you order the book for yourself and read in more detail what I am remarking on.

1.   Selection:
      a.   Coleman writes, "*His concern was not with programs to reach the multitudes, but with men whom the multitudes would follow. Remarkable as it may seem, Jesus started to gather these men before he ever organized an evangelistic campaign or even preached a sermon in public. Men were to be his method for winning the world to God.*"[20]
      b.   His selection process was unique. He didn't select men with marketing or theological backgrounds. He selected men

who were willing to learn. They were, as Dr. Howard Hendricks often said, *faithful, available,* and *teachable.* And they were leaders.

c.   He didn't choose many, but selected a few. This helped him to spend more time training each person.

d.   Be careful whom you choose to lead your kids. This is one of the most important steps to Jesus' strategy. Pick the right people to train and you will succeed. Pick the wrong people, and life will be hard for quite a while. Trust me. I have made that mistake.

2.   Association:

a.   Jesus spent time with his disciples. Training our leaders will take time. We will cover this more in chapter six on "Influencing the Influencers."

b.   "Knowledge was gained by association before it was understood by explanation."[21] *Showing* our leaders how to do something is more important than just *telling* them how to do it.

c.   "Jesus made it clear that before these men were 'to preach' or 'cast out devils' they were to be 'with him'."[22]

It is important for us, as leaders, to constantly encourage our volunteers to go deeper with Jesus *before* they come to our ministries to serve.

d.   It is our job to develop our leaders by associating with them on a regular basis, and to help new Christians have a Christian friend to associate with in order to continue the discipleship process.

3. Consecration:
   a. Jesus expected his disciples to obey him, even if they didn't understand him. They didn't have to be smart, just obedient.
   b. His teachings sometimes scared people away. The disciples had to count the cost of following him. We must also help our leaders understand that there will be sacrifices to serving. They must count the cost before saying yes to a leadership role.
   c. Jesus often demonstrated obedience to the Father so his disciples could see what obedience looked like. We, as leaders, must also demonstrate obedience to train our volunteers to do the same.
   d. What is God asking of you today that you have yet to yield obedience to? Delayed obedience is disobedience. Start obeying him now.

4. Impartation:
   a. Jesus gave himself away. We, too, must give of ourselves to our leaders. It is easier to follow your leader when they are transparent and open. Be this type of leader to your volunteers and they will follow you to the darkest parts of the world for God's glory.
   b. "His disciples were to give as freely as they had received. (Matt. 10:8) They were to love one another as he had loved them. (John 13:34-35)... Just as they had seen for three years, the disciples were to give themselves in selfless devotion to those whom the Father loved and for whom their Master died. (John 17:23)"23
   c. He promised, and eventually gave them, his Holy Spirit.
   d. He also imparted to them the mystery of the Gospel.

5. Demonstration
   a.   He showed them how to live. We talked about this earlier, but we are to have the same mind towards our volunteers as the Apostle Paul had towards his workers, when he said, "Imitate me as I imitate Christ." (1 Corinthians 11:1)
   b.   He taught his disciples how to pray and how to have closeness with the Father. He taught them that God could be called, "Abba."
   c.   He taught them how to read, interpret, and teach scripture.
   d.   Class was always in session. He used life to teach life. Every moment was a teachable moment. He demonstrated to his disciples how to see God's story in every situation.

6. Delegation:
   a.   He assigned them work. He gave his ministry away. We need to make sure we aren't asking our volunteers to just be "eyes" or "babysitters" for our events. Give them something significant to do.
   b.   Jesus had briefings with his disciples before they served. (Matt. 10:1; Mark 6:7; Luke 9:1,2) We will look at this more in the chapter six, but we should have a short, weekly huddle with our small group leaders before they serve each week.
   c.   The strategy included partners. Jesus sent the disciples out two-by-two. (Mark 6:7) One church has a saying that goes like this, "We never do ministry alone." They always have two people visit the hospital, or a home, together. No meeting has one church member with only one pastor. This might not be realistic for you or me in every situation, but I like the idea of it. This also helps in their discipleship process, because the older person is training one of the two.

7. Supervision:

    a.   He kept checking on them. We, as pastors, should constantly follow up on our leaders to see how they are doing--and what they might need in order to continue doing ministry.

    b.   Jesus would offer feedback when his disciples did ministry. (Matt. 17:14-20; Mark 9:17-29; Luke 9:37-43) Immediate feedback is the goal.

    c.   Jesus taught his disciples patience and unity. He corrected their thinking in regard to other people casting out demons in Jesus' name. (Mark 9:38; Luke 9:49) He said, *"Do not stop him, for whoever is not against you is for you."* (Luke 9:50)

8. Reproduction:

    a.   He expected them to reproduce. We, too, must have expectations for our leaders to actually perform the work of ministry. We must raise the bar of expectation for our volunteers.

    b.   Jesus knew his disciples had experienced his glory, and was confident that they would be effective witnesses for him.

    c.   After his earthly ministry was complete, Jesus gave his disciples his Great Commission. And this is where we are in the story.

I need to point out that Jesus used the same spiritual formation strategy we are proposing here. He invited his disciples to meet him during the selection process. For the disciples to follow him, they would have had to meet him for the first time. After the selection process, Jesus allowed them to get to know him better. As he spent time with them, they began to fall in love with him. And then he started delegating his ministry to them. The disciples went through the same spiritual formation you and I have gone through, and the same formation our kids will need to go through. Every student will need to meet Jesus, fall in love with Jesus, and serve Jesus. Now let's read Matthew 28:16-20. It is the Great Commission, and it is important for us to read together:

> *"Then the eleven disciples went to Galilee, to the mountain where Jesus had told them to go. When they saw him, they worshiped him; but some doubted. Then Jesus came to them and said, "All authority in heaven and on earth has been given to me. Therefore, go and make disciples of all nations, baptizing them in the name of the Father and the Son and the Holy Spirit, and teaching them to obey everything I have commanded you. And surely I am with you always to the very end of the age."*

In this passage, we see all three aspects to our spiritual formation plan: Meet Jesus. Fall in love with Jesus. Serve Jesus. *Therefore go and make disciples...* has the idea of people "serving Jesus". *Teaching them to obey* fits into the "fall in love with Jesus" category. *Baptizing them* is helping people "meet Jesus." It's all there. It's just backwards from what most churches do today. Dr. Barry St. Clair, in his training manual *"Jesus-focused Youth Ministry,"* encourages pastors to start with the end in mind. Even though he is focused on youth ministry, these principles apply to the church as a whole. There are six key aspects he points out. It all starts with us, as ministry leaders.

1. As leaders, we should go deeper in intimacy with Christ.
2. As leaders, we should pray with passion for God's presence and power.

3. As leaders, we should build volunteer leaders for in-depth and long-term ministry.
4. Then as leaders AND volunteer leaders, we should disciple kids to move toward maturity in Christ.
5. Then as leaders, volunteer leaders, and student leaders, we can penetrate the culture through relationships.
6. When the relationships are there and the leaders are in place, we create outreach opportunities to reach kids for Christ.[24]

Do you see how evangelism should not be the first thing on our minds? It should be the climax, or the natural outcome, of our ministry. As leaders, we must remember this truth. So let's finish this chapter by looking at a few ideas to help kids meet Jesus, fall in love with Jesus, and serve Jesus. Again, this is by no means an exhaustive list.

Helping kids meet Jesus, fall in love with Jesus, and serve Jesus

One of the main ways we try to help kids meet Jesus is what we shared in chapter three on our big group environment. Every week we keep in mind there might be a student in the crowd who has yet to follow Jesus. I always try to "land the plane" of my lesson facing towards the cross. What I mean by that is I try to show Jesus in every story of the Bible, whether it's a preschool lesson or a sermon for teens. (He's there. Help kids see that) Plus, it helps me move into some type of invitation each week.

A Case FOR Invitations

There seems to have been a move over the last few years in churches toward abandoning the invitation. I have never understood this. I was at a church plant one Sunday playing guitar for their service as a fill-in. Everything was great until the sermon was being finished. The music was good. The sermon was good. But immediately following the sermon, the pastor prayed, and then said, "Ok, well now we are going to take our morning offering." I thought that this was a strange place in the service timeline to put the offering. Immediately in between the sermon and the invitation? But after the offering was taken, the pastor dismissed us for the day.

Now, I know some of you might be thinking, "This guy is an old fart who likes *tradition* in the church." I am not fighting for *tradition*. I am fighting for the main purpose of what we do. If our purpose has anything to do with connecting kids to Jesus, or any number of variants of this, then there needs to be a moment when we *invite* kids to make a decision. So, I am not fighting for the old-school way of doing invitations where everyone stands up while the preacher adds a little guilt trip mini-sermon to manipulate people to move. But I'm not against a preacher pleading with people either, if done with a right heart. Peter and Paul pleaded with people; why shouldn't we? (Acts 2:40, Phil. 4:2)

My church has a normal invitation time, but it is a time to sing praises to the Lord in response to what he just taught us through his word. We have prayer partners in place for people to receive prayer and to make decisions. Call us "*old-school*", but I call us "*expectant*." We expect God to pierce hearts when his word is preached. What is the point of preaching if there is nothing we want the hearer to do because of the message? I'm not saying you have to give four stanzas of "*Just As I Am*" to have an invitation. What I am saying is we need to think about the *end* before we start. Ask yourself these questions before you finalize your next message: What's the point? What step do I want the hearers to take as a result of this lesson? Am I teaching this just to show how smart I am? Or is there a reason I feel the kids need to hear this information? If there is no reason for the kids to hear the information other than to know more Bible then it is a waste of their time. Remember what we shared earlier? The "win" for teaching is not education. The "win" is transformation. And if we don't invite them to do something then they are less likely to make any decision at all.

We need a new generation of ministry leaders who will begin inviting kids to meet Jesus for the first time, to go deeper by committing to spiritual disciplines (fall in love with Jesus), and we need leaders to bring back the invitation aspect of kids feeling called to missions or vocational ministry (serve Jesus).

Since my family ministry has life groups for our high school kids on Wednesday nights after our big group sermon we use the life group as the invitation. We preach every message *towards* the small group. In other words, we try and leave the message open-ended so the small group leaders can easily continue the conversation in their groups. Plus, if there are any decisions that need to be made, it can be done in the small group--where the student will have immediate love, support, and discipleship.

Depending on your age level of ministry, your format may not allow for this to happen, but you should still prioritize the invitation. Think creatively about how you can give kids real and meaningful times to reflect on what God just taught them. Help make it clear what the next step is for them, if they want to make a decision.

A Case for Outreach Events
(Help kids meet Jesus)

In the past, and in the present, too many churches have relied on the outreach events for numerical growth and have found their resources spent on big events with little to no lasting impact. Remember what Dr. St. Clair said earlier? "When the relationships are there and the leaders are in place, *THEN* we create outreach opportunities to reach kids for Christ."

The churches that are less successful in their outreach efforts are those with no foundation in place to properly disciple new converts. These churches focus on evangelism first. However, this doesn't mean outreach events are never important. Just be sure to let evangelism be the natural fruit of your ministry and not the only focus. Then, once this principle/structure is in place, be strategic in your outreach events.

Here are a few ideas to help you plan:

1. Use dates where you will already have a large crowd. Some churches try to schedule outreach events on days when numbers are historically low in order to entice kids to show up. This strategy wastes resources. If your church is like mine you only have so much money to go

around. *Make it count.* Look at your attendance records and see when you had the highest attendance on a regular week. Use *that* week to host an outreach event.

2. Use Wednesday nights, or whenever you do your "big group" gathering, for outreach. Kids are showing up anyway, and this will train them to invite friends on your "big group" night throughout the year. Plus, this is more parent-friendly since most kids can't drive. Also, guests will be able to get a glimpse into your normal programing. If a student makes a decision at the outreach event, it will be easier to transition them from the outreach event to your normal weekly "big group."

3. As much as possible, let your kids have some input into the event. Let them plan a certain aspect. People support what they have helped to create. Delegate. Delegate. Delegate.

4. Quality is key. Don't throw something together last minute. Plan. Plan. Plan.

5. No one will respond to the gospel if no one shows up. Figure out creative ways to get the word out about the event. Advertise. Advertise. Advertise.

6. It's all about Jesus being lifted up. Be sure there is a clear gospel message and a way for kids to respond. Preach. Preach. Preach.

7. The most important thing to do is pray. Lee Strobel once said, "Before you talk to your friends about God, talk to God about your friends." Pray. Pray. Pray.

A Case for Follow-up
(Help kids fall in love with Jesus)

There is a real need in church today for follow-up. After an outreach event, most kids who make decisions simply fall through the cracks and are forgotten. This is not good. Remember, Jesus never said for us to make converts. He wants disciples. It is our job to make sure we follow-up on all decisions made at our gatherings. If a decision is made at one of our weekly groups, it should be easy to follow-up. Have the leader from the life group the student should attend (or already attends) get in touch with them. Getting kids plugged into a circle is so important for the discipleship of new believers. Have a short study available for older kids or adults to walk through with the new believer. The study should help them understand the basic truths of Christianity. Don't make this a long study. A 13-week study or longer can be scary for a new believer.

At my church we have a four-session study for new believers. We say, *"We are so excited you decided to follow Jesus! We have a four-week study we'd love to walk you through in order to help you better understand the decision you just made."* In our family ministry we have several older kids and adults who, at any time, could lead these studies. They are always prepared. We actually do the sessions one-on-one or one-on-three during the Sunday morning life group hours. We do this because they are more than likely already going to be there. And we don't feel like four weeks away from the life group will harm them. They are building a deeper relationship with an older Christian and learning more about God's word.

At the end of the four weeks we give them a "quiet time" journal to help them continue the discipline of Bible study--and we make sure they are plugged into a life group. Discipleship continues through the life group. This is a great way to help kids who just met Jesus to *fall in love with him.*

A Case for Worship One. Serve One.
(Help kids serve Jesus)

After helping kids meet Jesus, we need to help them fall in love with him. I believe as kids fall more deeply in love with Jesus, they will naturally want to serve him. So, let's help them serve more than once a year at a mission trip, or a couple of times per year on a service project. Let's help them serve every week. I heard Doug Fields give an illustration in a sermon recently about high school kids' desire to serve. This is what he shared,

Kids respond to God in different ways at different phases and they need various approaches from us to help them move towards maturity during each phase. It's like going to Disney World. Preschool kids will walk into the entrance and be content there. Mickey and Goofy will both be there. The entrance is all a preschooler needs to be happy. But as they get older and enter into the children's ministry they are no longer content to just hang out in the entrance. They want to go explore the park. And as they move into middle school they want to continue to explore the park. But now they want to ride all the rides. As they enter high school they want to continue to ride the rides, but now they want to operate them. So, let high school teenagers operate the rides!

His point was that high school kids are interested in helping operate the church *now*. They don't want to wait until they are an "adult" to lead. They want to lead now. So, why not partner them with a loving adult mentor and give them responsibilities within the church each week? Churches are constantly in need of capable volunteers, yet they are sitting on a treasure chest full of completely capable young adults in the student ministry. These kids are ready to serve--if only they were allowed. Let them help with the first impressions team who greet in the parking lot or at the doors. Preschoolers and children LOVE high school kids. This is also a great way to teach your preschool and children what service looks like and what will be expected of them, as they get older. You will have to pick and choose the right kids to serve in these areas, and there will need to be some child protection training, but treat teenagers the same as you would treat an adult. Walk them through the process to volunteer. Kids will respect you for doing this, and they will feel like you treated them like an adult.

And as kids enter high school they need fewer conversations and more action in their lives. High school kids will never feel important until you give them something important to do.[25]

We moved our high school life groups from Sunday to Wednesday for several reasons, but one of the major reasons was to free their Sundays up so the teens could serve weekly. We call this "Worship One. Serve One." We did not come up with the name. Many churches are already doing this better than we are, but we have loved this program. The idea is, since they have life groups on another day, we will let them choose which worship service they want to attend. Then we will encourage them to serve during the hour they used to have life groups. Every Sunday they will worship one hour and serve one hour. They will possibly be some of your best volunteers. Here is the best part:

Your adults will love seeing kids serve.

Think about the little old lady walking up to the church. The door is opened and a handsome young gentleman grabs her hand and helps her down the hall to her classroom. Maybe the coffee never tasted quite as good before, since there is now a lovely young lady at the coffee bar smiling at every adult she hands the cup to. Imagine the church becoming more tech savvy, simply because teenagers are helping with the marketing and production of the services. Or there are more musicians to choose from now that kids are allowed to serve during the first service, instead of sitting in a classroom. The volunteer positions are limited only to your own creativity.

"I am WITH you"

In verse 20 of Matthew 28 we see the last words of the Great Commission: *"And surely I am with you always, to the very end of the age."* Jesus knew the disciples would be scared. Have you ever been scared to try new things? Scared of change? The truth is some people won't like the idea of kids serving on Sunday morning. Or they won't like the idea of other changes you might make as a result of this book. And, because of this, you might be afraid to try new things due to the potential fallout you might encounter. Jesus understands. That is why he said, "I will be *with you.*"

I use to be afraid of the dark. Well, I guess I still am afraid of the dark. I work at a church and there are times I have to stay late to lock up. There are certain places in the church that are darker than others. I'm just being honest here. When I walk through the really dark places, I start to walk a little faster.

I remember when I was a boy; my father and I would hunt with dogs late at night. We would be in the middle of a field on a pitch-black night with all kinds of scary noises around us. But for some reason, I am still more scared in a dark hallway by myself today than I was in a dark field at the age of 10. Why? I had my father with me. That's all I needed. If my dad was with me, I could go anywhere and I could do anything. I relied on my father's strength and not my own. Jesus says, "I will be *with you*" to give us the same confidence I had when I was with my earthly father. So, don't be afraid. Jesus will do his ministry *through* us if we just submit to his will. And life will never be the same!

(Recap Reading Experience)

Spiritual formation is simply helping kids meet Jesus for the first time, helping them fall in love with him by getting to know him better, and helping them begin to serve him. We believe it starts with us, as pastors. What makes the Great Commission so GREAT? Jesus chooses to *let us participate* in God's story. He invites us in the same way he invited his original disciples: Meet me. Fall in love with me. Serve me. Evangelism was not the first thing on Jesus' mind. It was the climax, or the natural outcome, of his ministry. As we go deeper with intimacy with Jesus, pray with passion for God's presence and power, build leaders for ministry, disciple kids to move toward maturity, penetrate the culture through relationships, and create outreach opportunities, we will see more kids meet Jesus, fall in love with Jesus, and serve Jesus for the rest of their lives. Now *that* is a life worth living.

TWO PRIORITIES
CHAPTER 6

Influencing the Influencers

An important principle in ministry is the principle of the iceberg. The iceberg is a perfect picture of why most churches are not making a significant impact in the world around them. Only about 10% of an iceberg is visible above the surface. Roughly 90% is underneath the surface and is rarely ever seen. But, as we learned from the story of the Titanic, what's underneath the surface sinks ships.

Too often, ministry leaders focus only on the top 10% and neglect the bottom 90%. We tend to be so concerned with glitter and glamour that we neglect what matters most. Too often we struggle with the temptation of wanting to make more of an *impression* than an *impact*. We want to be known as the cool, hip church in town, so we give more attention to what is seen than what is not seen. However, the bottom 90% determines whether or not our ministry will be truly successful.

Everything we have covered so far in this book has been the tip of the iceberg, or the things people see. But for the remaining chapters, I want to spend some time talking about the things most people never see. In order for us to help kids meet Jesus, fall in love with Jesus, and serve Jesus through big group and small group experiences, we need to influence more people than just the children or teenagers we serve. We need to influence the *influencers* of our kids. There are two institutions God has established for discipleship: the family and the church. So, it is our job to protect and strengthen both in order to do what God has set them up to do. We will be looking at how we can influence both institutions for the good of the kids we serve.

The Family

The family: God's first institution. Genesis 1:26 says, *"Then God said, 'Let us make man in our image, in our likeness..."* The next verse says, *"Then God made mankind in his own image, in the image of God he created them; male and female he created them."* God told Adam and Eve to *"be fruitful and multiply; fill the earth and subdue it. Rule over the fish in the sea and the birds in the sky and over every living creature that moves on the ground."* (Genesis 1:28) Genesis 2:24 says, *"For this reason a man will leave his father and mother and be united to his wife and the two will become one flesh."* God set up, from the beginning, the family unit to be his method of service and discipleship to the world. I heard Dr. Richard Ross give an example in a sermon once. He said,

> *"Let's say, for a moment, that I were to ask everybody who was involved in the preschool and children's ministry of the church to stand on one side of the stage; if you help on Wednesday nights or Sunday mornings. Perhaps you can only help during VBS or camp. Now, I continue to ask those who help with student ministry to also stand with them. Whether Wednesday night helpers or Sunday morning teachers, disciple now leaders, camp and other special events. I suspect there would be a large group of people on one side of the stage. Now, on the other side of the stage, I ask for a mom and a dad to stand here. Which side of the stage has the greatest potential impact on the life of a child or teenager? I would have to say the mom and the dad!"*

I want to ask you a few questions:

1. How many of you ever thought to yourself, "I'm never going to turn into my parents"?
2. How many of you, if you were honest, would say that in a lot of ways you DID turn into your parents?

It's scary isn't it? I mean, when I was a child I thought my parents were geniuses. Yet, when I became a teenager I thought they were nuts. Now that I am an adult, I realize I am just like they were. We tend to inherit the same mannerisms as our parents. We walk like they walk. We talk like they talk. We say the same things to our children that they used to say to us. *"If you don't stop crying, I'm going to give you something to cry about."* (As a child, I never understood what they meant. I already had something to cry about. That's why I was crying.) But as an adult with kids, I can see where they were coming from. The truth is--our parents influence us all, for better or for worse.

In fact, research and scripture agree: parents have the potential to be the *primary* spiritual influence in the lives of their kids. What this means is, as parents, we cannot drop our kids off at church and expect *our* faith to pass on to them. Our spiritual convictions, for better or worse, will most always pass from parent to child, not pastor to child.

In truly one of the best books on this subject, *reThink*, Steve Wright shares some interesting quotes that I feel are appropriate to share here. He challenges his readers to guess where the following quotes are from:

1. *"Studies have shown that parents are the primary influence on their children's choices and decisions...and that is why we're proud to offer help to parents. Recognizing that parents have the greatest influence on their children's decisions, the Family Talk program helps...by encouraging open, honest communication between parents and children."*

2. *"Nearly three out of four parents believe their children's friends and classmates have the most influence...Yet contrary to what parents think, kids say mom and dad have the biggest impact on the choices they make."*

3. *"So you're between the ages of 13 and 24. What makes you happy? A worried, weary parent might imagine the answer to sound something like this: sex, drugs, and a little rock 'n' roll. Maybe some cash, or at least the car keys. Turns out the real answer is quite different. Spending time with family was the top answer to that open-ended question...Parents are seen as an overwhelmingly positive influence in the lives of most young people. Remarkably, nearly half of teens mention at least one of the parents as a hero."*

Ready for the answers? The first quote was from an Anheuser-Busch publication on one of their past websites called Family Talk Online. The second quote was from a website of the Coors Brewing company called MVParenting. The third quote was from a study conducted by MTV and the Associated Press. Whether it's a Christian organization or a very worldly one, all research points to the fact that parents are the primary influence of their children. Parents are primary."[26] So it seems pretty clear from research that parents are the most influential people to their children, in every area including spirituality. But this

shouldn't surprise us. This is God's design. Read with me
Deuteronomy 6:4-9:

> *"Hear, O Israel: The LORD our God, the LORD is one. Love*
> *the LORD your God with all your heart and with all your*
> *soul and with all your strength. These commandments that I*
> *give you today are to be on your hearts. Impress them on*
> *your children. Talk about them when you sit at home and*
> *when you walk along the road, when you lie down and when*
> *you get up. Tie them as symbols on your hands and bind them*
> *on your foreheads. Write them on the doorframes of your*
> *houses and on your gates."*

Many people believe the most well known scripture in the Bible is
John 3:16, but it's not. Deuteronomy 6:4-9 is what the Jewish people
call the Great Shema. It is the most quoted scripture in the world.
Jewish families quote this passage by memory every morning and
evening. It was designed to be a constant reminder to the Jewish
people of their role, as parents, in the discipleship process. Parents are
God's "Plan A" for discipleship. Everything else is "Plan B." The
church should desire to partner with God's "Plan A" by giving parents
resources, training opportunities, and other help in the discipleship of
their kids. We cannot guarantee godly parents in the lives of each
student, but we can be a resource for the family.

We, as leaders, should help parents in the church understand that what
happens at home is more impactful than what happens at church.[27]
This does not mean that what happens at the church doesn't matter. It
just means that our spiritual convictions, for better or worse, will most
always pass from parent to child, not pastor to child. You don't have
to like this truth, but don't put your head in the sand and ignore it.

So, if this is really true, then our focus on ministry should change drastically. Dr. Ross wrote an incredible blog called, *"Less Traditional Student Ministry might mean more disciples."*[28] The article applies to preschool and children's ministry leaders as well. In it, he writes about how traditional ministry has proven to be less effective than we had once hoped. Traditionally, the ministry leader focused most, if not all, of his or her time reaching out to and discipling kids. But with new research suggesting the influence of the parents, Ross suggests we recalculate our weekly hours to include the following:

1. Approximately 15 hours a week accelerating the spiritual impact of the homes where our kids live.

2. Approximately 15 hours a week immersing every kid in the full life and ministry of the congregation.

3. Approximately 15 hours a week leading what we traditionally have considered ministry.

I am aware that many of you reading this right now might be saying, "I am bi-vocational, or part time, or a volunteer. I wish I had 15 hours a week to devote to the ministry." Well, don't miss his point. Don't look at the hours in the example as much as the percentage of time. However much time you typically devote to the ministry, Ross is saying you should give 33% to educating/partnering with parents, 33% to helping kids be actively involved in the whole church, and 33% to what is considered "traditional" ministry. So, if we truly want to influence the children we serve with the gospel of Jesus Christ, we have to face the fact that we MUST partner with parents.

Reggie Joiner, in his book, *Think Orange*, shares that the average church has only 40 hours a year to influence a life.[29] He bases that number on the reality that many kids attend just one hour per week, for 40 weeks out of 52 weeks. I would hope that we could do better, and so I will be optimistic and say we can get *some* kids to church TWO times per week for 45 weeks out of the year. This gives us 90 hours per year with a child. Now, let's see how much time a parent has each year with the same child. The average parent has 3,000 hours per year to influence a life. Math lesson: 3,000 is greater than 90.

Let's not fool ourselves into thinking we can compete with parents. Think about it for a moment. Haven't there been times in your ministry where you said to yourself, "That kid would be on fire for the Lord *if it weren't for their parents.*" Early in my ministry I didn't like parents that much. (Am I allowed to say this?) I thought parents were hindering my ministry. But now I know this truth:

Parents weren't hindering MY ministry; I was really hindering THEIR ministry!

And it is time for ministry leaders to fix this terrible way of thinking. Now that we understand our need to influence the parent, let's talk briefly about HOW to influence well. This is by no means an exhaustive list of things we should do to partner with parents, but it will help get us started in the right direction.

Partnering with Parents

Parents are people, too. And that means they make mistakes and get scared of the unknown like anybody else. The truth is: most parents, even the ones you think couldn't care less about their kids, want to succeed at raising their children. They are actually terrified they are going to ruin their kids' future by how they parent. They may not understand this, but they are scared because they have never parented before. And the church has often been guilty of making parents feel bad for not knowing what we, as spiritual leaders, have never taught them to know in the first place-- how to be the spiritual leader of the family. Dr. Tim Kimmel, in his book, *Connecting Church & Home*, gives this definition of the family and the church:

- Family: The Domestic Church
- Church: A gathering of Domestic Churches[30]

Someone might argue with Kimmel, saying that to be a member of a church you have to be a Christian. To be sure, there are many families where members are as lost as a helium balloon in a thunderstorm. But I still agree with his point. Dr. Kimmel is trying to help us see God's original design for discipleship for the next generation rests in the family. Of course, we know that sin wrecked the effectiveness of this plan. However, if we begin to see the family as a domestic church, we will better understand the church-collective's role in the discipleship process. What if we started recognizing our responsibility, as spiritual leaders, was to empower and equip the family to continue at home what the church teaches in our gatherings? If we did, the spiritual conversations would continue from Sunday to Monday, Tuesday, Wednesday...etc. Parents need to be reminded of their role as primary spiritual leaders of their kids discipleship--but they will never know this truth if we don't get out of their way and encourage them to do it. They need to be educated on how little time they have, and how to maximize the time they have, for the glory of God.

Parenting Lessons from the Patriots?

If you missed Super Bowl LI, you missed one of the most incredible games in NFL history. It was the greatest comeback story in Super Bowl history and was the first time any NFL coach had won five Super Bowl rings. It was the first time in fifty years a Super Bowl went into overtime. No matter how you feel about the Patriots, you had to respect them that night. They earned that win.

I think, as parents, we can learn a lesson from that game. By the middle of the 3rd quarter, the Falcons had an impressive lead of 28-3, and it looked like all hope was lost for the Patriots. No team had ever come back from more than a ten-point deficit in any previous Super Bowl. They could have easily given up and gone home. But they didn't. They came back to win in overtime and proved to the world one simple truth: NEVER QUIT!

As parents, there are times when we want to quit speaking words of hope and start speaking words of disappointment. There are times when we look at our preschooler and ask, *"Is it too late to send that one back for a refund?"* I have spoken with many parents who have major regrets for the way they raised their kids in the first half of their lives, and they recognize that the teen years are harder simply because the first half wasn't played to the best of their ability.

Below is my version of a graphic found in the revolutionary book, *It's Just a Phase, so Don't Miss It* by Joiner and Ivy, which I've already mentioned before. I don't get paid telling you this, but you need this book on your shelf and in your head.

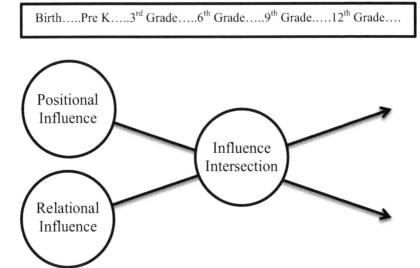

Birth.....Pre K.....3rd Grade.....6th Grade.....9th Grade.....12th Grade....

Positional Influence

Relational Influence

Influence Intersection

In this graphic, we see the difference between positional influence and relational influence. If you will notice, the influence parents have over their child from the time they are born to the time they enter middle school is called "Positional Influence." They have influence over their child simply because of the *position* they hold as parent. But once the child enters middle school, the second half of play begins. If parents are not careful, they will not make any halftime adjustments to the game plan and will lose influence over their teens. The church must warn and inform moms and dads this change is coming.

Also, we must encourage and support those who think it's too late. Parents must build "relational *credit*" during the first half of their child's life so they will have "relational *equity*" during the second half. But even if they played the first half of their child's life poorly, there's still hope. We can, and should, encourage parents to begin making halftime adjustments to their parenting and start building a relationship with their teen.

The way you spell love to a teenager is "T-I-M-E". Start spending quality time with them. Start praying for/with them. Start speaking words of affirmation to them. No matter how the first half was played, it's always the second half that determines whether you win or lose.

Parents need constant reminders to take a lesson from the Patriots and never give up, make appropriate halftime adjustments, and watch their teen thrive towards victory. Parents also need to know that the church is here to partner with them in every phase of their child's life. Joiner would also encourage church leaders to reactivate parents by:

- Creating a content calendar with everything you want parents to know.
- Organizing a plan to cue parents weekly with key information when they need it.
- Establishing annual parent orientations to equip them for the next phase.
- Recruiting leaders to connect with every parent, especially those who never show up.
- Providing resources to enhance family time in the home.

A great way to "cue" the parent is to set them up for success in having spiritual conversations at home. One way to do this is to have a weekly communications of some kind, whether it is an email or a text, informing parents of what you are teaching their child. Providing conversation starters that reinforce your lesson is a great way to help parents continue the conversation at home.

Another great way is to have a life group for parents that you, or a trusted parent, teach each week. Have this class teach through the same scripture/curriculum you will use for your kids. Teach the parents the lesson *BEFORE* you teach the kids, and give the parents suggested conversation starters to help them have spiritual conversations at home. For example, if you have the opportunity to have a Sunday morning life group for parents, you can teach them the lesson you are teaching their children on Wednesday. Parents will then be equipped with a better understanding of scripture, will have a conversation starter ready for their kid, and will be able to continue the conversation you will start with their child that coming week. This will help the lesson "go home."

Lessons that go home are more likely to be lived out.

These are just a few ways to begin to partner with parents in the discipleship process. I am NOT an advocate of abandoning the church's role in the discipleship of students, but I do feel that for us to truly make a lasting impact, we will need to partner with the parents. Now that we have talked briefly about influencing the first institution God established, let's spend the rest of this chapter on the second institution: the Church.

The Church

The church: God's second institution. Jesus mentions the impact the church would soon have on the world when he said in Matthew 16:18, *"...I will build my church, and the gates of Hades will not overcome it."* My pastor once preached a message on this passage. He said the interesting truth about this passage is that gates in bible times were always used to keep people *out*. So when Jesus said the gates of Hades would not overcome, he was implying something that we miss too often. When we read this passage, we tend to think that Hades is on the offense and we are on the defense. But if this were true, then Jesus would have said, "the gates of *Heaven* would not *be* overcome" since gates were meant to keep something or someone *out*. In other words, if Hades were on the offense, then we would be on the defense. Since we know that gates were designed to keep people out, when Jesus says that Hades will not overcome, we know he is expecting the church to not be on defense, but offense. Too many churches are living in a state of defense. Jesus calls us to storm the gates of Hell because the gates will not overcome the power of the cross!

In Acts chapters one and two when Jesus pours out his Holy Spirit on the believers at Pentecost, he establishes his church. And in Acts 1:8, he tells them to be active in being witnesses to the whole world. The church is the second institution he commissions to bring discipleship to the world. He gave them, and us, his great commission and expects us to be on the offense for the kingdom. Let's get busy making disciples.

Since we have already talked about our role at influencing the first
influencer, the family, I want to spend this time talking about our job,
as leaders, at influencing the second influencer, the church. And when
I say "church", I mean those within the church. If we are going to
succeed at influencing kids, we will have to succeed at influencing
parents AND church members to volunteer. By the way, parents make
incredible volunteers. They already know the kids, love the kids, and
want you to succeed. If you succeed, their kids succeed. Plus, this is
just another way to partner with parents.

Volunteer Care

Family ministry must be excellent at volunteer recruitment and
volunteer retention. I don't know about your budget, but my budget
won't pay for all the staff we need for our family ministry. This is
why family ministry, as well as the rest of the church, must rely
heavily on volunteers. But how do we recruit volunteers? How do we
train them? And how do we retain them? The best book I have read
on this subject is by Darren Kizer, Christine Kreisher, and Steph
Whitacre called, *The Volunteer Project: Stop Recruiting, Start
Retaining.* In this book, they dream of having a "zero recruitment"
future where ministries are taking such good care of the volunteers
they have that there is no need for the leaders to recruit any more
volunteers. Now, that has been my dream since I started ministry. But
how do they propose we actually do this? Below is a short summary
of the book, but I would highly encourage you to buy it and read it
several times. So here is a summary of *"The Volunteer Project: Stop
Recruiting, Start Retaining."* Volunteer *retention* always trumps

volunteer *recruitment*. It takes exponentially more energy to recruit a new volunteer than to retain an existing one.[31] The book is based on four mindsets every leader should have:

- Excellence: People don't want to be part of something that isn't done with excellence. Do the best you can with what you have.
- Mission: Be sure the purpose, or mission, is easy to understand and meaningful. People want to be part of something bigger than them.
- Appreciation: The "salary" for any volunteer is the *appreciation* they receive for a job well done. In order to retain volunteers, you must regularly esteem them for what they are doing for the kingdom.
- Invitation: Irresistible invitations are marked by opportunity, not desperation, and are unapologetic in nature. Show new recruits the magnitude of the job they will be volunteering for. They want to live *UP* to something greater than themselves.

As leaders, we should cast a great vision of what we are asking our volunteers to be part of. As Reggie Joiner would say, "Help them see that:

- It's not babysitting, it's discipleship.
- It's not pizza, it's a relationship.
- It's not a party, it's a platform.
- It's not filling a volunteer spot, it's influencing someone's future."[32]

Help volunteers find their sweet spot. The goal is not to fill a position; the goal is to get the right people on the bus, then get them in the right seat on the bus. So how do you retain volunteers? Help them find their sweet spot and they will stay with you for a very long time.

Leaders need to show the *value* of the volunteer ministry. Show volunteers how much money the church would have to spend if they had to staff every volunteer position. Kizer states,

> *"When I realize volunteers have given 'donations' of time amounting to nearly $50,000 of personnel time, I am incredibly grateful for what is given. When is the last time you opened a letter with a $50,000 donation enclosed? Imagine that donation arriving every week accompanied by smiles and stories of life change."*[33]

Leaders should always be open and approachable. Constantly be tweaking your ministry and allow volunteers' input into the evaluation process. Remember, people will support what they have helped to create. Be sure to show appreciation often. *"Think of appreciation as a volunteer's paycheck. What would you do if you were hired for your dream job, but after a few months, you stopped receiving a paycheck? I'm going to assume you might not stay at that job much longer."*[34]

Leaders should know the importance of training for success. When a potential volunteer is approached about serving, there should be a clear process in place to get them trained and on the team.

Here's an example:

1. Explore his or her interests.
2. Have the potential volunteer observe in his or her area of interest *BEFORE* serving.
3. Provide a link to, or physical copies of, necessary paperwork (application, background check forms, etc.).
4. Complete background check and reference checks.
5. Welcome new volunteer on team and begin the orientation. Describe the policies and procedures. Give clear expectations for attendance and participation. Give your contact info and have Q&A with volunteer.
6. Implement a training process in which new volunteers shadow you or another experienced volunteer.
   a. Week #1: I do, you watch.
   b. Week #2: I do, you help.
   c. Week #3: You do, I help.
   d. Week #4: You do, I watch.
   e. Week #5: You do!
7. Make intentional contact on weeks #4 and #8
8. Check in periodically.[35]

Never host a "meeting." Host a "huddle" where the team huddles for a few minutes before each week's big group or small group experience. Give them something for the hand (appropriate discussion guides, attendance sheets, etc.), give them something for the head (announcements and reminders), and give them something for the heart (a quick inspirational story to keep them motivated and focused on the task at hand).[36]

Leaders need to communicate early and often. Be responsible with your leaders and respect them enough to give them a head's up well in advance of upcoming events and curriculum. As the team grows, organize in such a way as to have "Coaches" for teams of volunteers, so each volunteer has someone to give support. Also, help volunteers become a family. Some volunteers will be missing out on life groups. Let their volunteer team be the *community* they are missing in life group. Let their team be a safe place to belong.

As volunteers become friends and have fun, they will become the best recruiting agents for new volunteers. Be sure to calendar times for you, as the leader, to take volunteers out to lunch or coffee. Also, calendar training times and team parties. Make each training time fun and informative. Finally, release them to do what God has empowered them to do. Give away the ministry.

Again, this is a *very* brief summary of the text. I would encourage you to purchase this book and read it with your staff. You will not regret this investment. It will change your ministry forever. By influencing these influencers, volunteers, you will see your ministry impact soar and your stress will recede. You will enjoy the ministry more and will find that your physical, as well as spiritual, health is at its peak.

(Recap Reading Experience)

If we truly want to have a lasting impact with children and youth, we must realize that influencing ONLY kids is not the answer. We must influence the influencers. God ordained the family AND the church to be the primary means for discipleship in the world. Parents and volunteers are the influencers most capable of making a significant impact in the spiritual growth of the kids God has entrusted to our care. As leaders, we must constantly be looking for opportunities to train, inform, encourage, equip, and influence the influencers in order to maximize what little bit of time we have with our kids. Nothing is worth more than influencing the next generation for Christ. Legacies are born this way.

ONE PERSON
CHAPTER 7

It's All About Jesus

In view of a call: In the Baptist denomination, there is a process for finding new pastors when a church is pastor-less. The church assigns a group of trusted individuals to serve on a "pastor search team" in order to weed through the hundreds of resumes from potential candidates to determine who might be a great fit for their setting. After a pastor search team finds a person of interest, meets with them, and interviews them many times, they will recommend that person to the church as a potential pastor. The church will then ask the person to come preach "In View of a Call." The church will meet the prospective pastor and his family, hear him preach, and then vote on whether or not they would like to call him to their church as the next pastor.

There is another way we can look at the phrase, "In View of a Call." It is more personal, between the individual and God himself. But it is NOT the individual who is doing the calling. God is the one calling and, for every believer reading this today, there is a calling God has placed on your life. It is your life call. Every believer has been given a specific purpose by God and is held accountable every day as to how he or she is doing *in view of the call.*

When God called me at the age of 15 to full-time ministry I had a wrong view of the call. I viewed the call through human lenses and not in light of the one doing the calling. I knew what I wanted and full-time ministry was not it. Not only did I have a distorted view of the *call*, but also I had a distorted view of the *Caller.* I viewed God as a cosmic Santa Claus waiting to give me what I wanted and to get me out of a jam from time to time. He was nothing more than my genie in a bottle, ready to grant me any wish I desired. But, if he was a genie in a bottle and I was the one holding the bottle what did that make me? His master.

There is a biblical character that perfectly illustrates this. We are going to look at the whole book of Jonah. (Don't freak out. It's only four chapters. And we will do more of a summary than an in-depth study).

The Story of Jonah Examined

The book begins with the word of the Lord coming to Jonah. God tells Jonah to go to Nineveh and preach against it, because its wickedness has come up before the Lord. But Jonah ran from the Lord.

Right off the bat, Jonah hears from God and disobeys. Spoiler alert: we find out in the final chapter why Jonah ran from the Lord. It was NOT because he was afraid of the Ninevites, but because he hated them. Nineveh was the capital city of Assyria. Assyria was a ruthless enemy of Israel. Before Rome perfected crucifixion, Assyria perfected the art of skinning people alive. They were evil and harsh.

So yes, Jonah might have been a bit scared to preach against Nineveh. However, fear was not his main motive for disobeying God. He hated the Assyrians and wanted them to perish. So we see him run from the Lord and head to Tarshish in the opposite direction. It would seem like Jonah thought he could actually remove himself from the Lord's presence. This is the first clue that Jonah had a vision problem. He had a small view of God. Also, prophets were God's instruments to speak God's message to the people on God's behalf. Jonah's main job as a prophet was to hear from God and speak what he heard. He was to be God's mouthpiece to the world. Jonah, however, thought he had the right to choose which messages he would preach and which messages he would repress. So, he had a small view of God and a big view of Jonah.

You know the story. Jonah runs away from the mission. God sends a storm. The sailors cast lots to see who is the cause of the storm. Jonah confesses and is thrown overboard. The storm stops. A great fish swallows up Jonah and he smells really bad for at least three days. I would think this might change Jonah's view of the call just a bit. And it does. Jonah's view of God becomes bigger and his view of himself becomes smaller. He cries out to God, and God has the great fish spit Jonah up on the shore. The word of the Lord comes to Jonah a second time--and Jonah obeys. This is encouraging for you and for me. As the Veggie tales movie about Jonah so accurately communicates in a song, "God is a God of second chances". So, Jonah obeys and goes to Nineveh to preach against it, and the people hear the message and repent. From the top down, Nineveh repents of their ways and gets right with God. In a massive, citywide revival, the whole city gets saved. Jonah must be so excited...right? Wrong. The beginning of chapter four says,

"But to Jonah this seemed very wrong, and he became angry. He prayed to the Lord, 'Isn't this what I said, Lord, when I was still at home? This is what I tried to forestall by fleeing to Tarshish. I knew that you were a gracious and compassionate God; slow to anger and abounding in love, a God who relents from sending calamity. Now, Lord, take away my life, for it is better for me to die than to live.' But the Lord replied, "Is it right for you to be angry?"'"

Jonah doesn't even answer God's question. Instead, he leaves the city and sits on a hill; watching and hoping God might still destroy the people Jonah had just seen come to God. Jonah gets hot and tired and makes a shelter for himself. He is trying to get a good seat to watch the destruction. Once again, Jonah has a small view of God and a big view of Jonah. He has a distorted view of the call. Plus, did you notice how racist Jonah was? Have you ever hated a different nationality so much that you truly wanted them to die a horrible death? This is a "man of God" and he would rather see someone die than to come to God. He even screams at God and pretty much says,

"I knew you were a good God. That's why I didn't want to go to Nineveh. I knew that if they would turn to you then you would forgive them. I hated them so much I wanted to withhold information from them so that they would die and go to Hell. God! You ruined my plan!" (Preston Paraphrase)

In a real sense, Jonah was trying to *be* God. He was trying to be the one to choose who receives grace and who doesn't. All the while God is showing *him* grace after grace. (It reminds me of the parable of the "unmerciful servant" in Matthew 18:21-35.) God is gracious to Jonah and gives him a "leafy plant" to give him relief from the sun, and Jonah is happy. But the next day God sends a worm to eat the plant and make it wither. Jonah complains again that he'd rather die than live. God then answers him and asks, *"Is it right for you to be angry about this plant?"* Notice how God asks the same question in a different context. *"Is it right for you to be angry...?"* (4:4, 4:9) Jonah shows us once again his distorted view of the God of the universe when he says, *"It is! I am so angry I wish I were dead."* #whatababy!

Then God concludes the book with a really strange ending. He says,

"You have been concerned about this plant, though you did not tend it or make it grow. It sprang up overnight and died overnight. And should I not have concern for the great city of Nineveh, in which there are more than a hundred and twenty thousand people who cannot tell their right hand from their left--and also many animals?"

And that is the conclusion of the book. What a lousy ending. It's almost as if the writer wanted to leave the reader with this uncomfortable interlude between what *is* and what *should be*. God speaks. Jonah disobeys. God disciplines. Jonah obeys. God blesses. Jonah gets mad. God speaks again. The end. Now what? Where is the prophetic message from God to his people? Where is the resolution of the story? Where is the closure?

The Story of Jonah Explained

Here is the secret to understanding the message of this book: the story of Jonah *IS* the message of God to his people. The people of God had a distorted view of the call of God on their lives. They believed they were more important than all other nations simply because God had chosen them to be his people. But if you will remember, God chose them for a specific purpose. It wasn't that God loved Israel more than any other nation. Clearly God cared about the people of Nineveh too. Israel was not called by God to sit in the blessings of being "God's people" without doing anything for the rest of the world. God expected Israel to be his light to a lost world in order to bring all nations back to God. (See verses about Israel's purpose in Appendix four of this book.)

There are many verses that inform us of the purposes of Israel. They were *blessed* to be a *blessing*. They were called to be the light to the nations, so the nations would know who the only true God is. God called them, not to *salvation*, but to a *purpose*. That purpose was to proclaim God to the nations and to make Him famous. And, just like Jonah in the story, Israel was not fulfilling their God-given call. They had a distorted view of the call and of the One doing the calling. Jonah was a representative of Israel. So, the story of Jonah *IS* the story of Israel. When God spoke to Jonah he was actually speaking to Israel.

When the Lord replied, "*Is it right for you to be angry?*" he was actually saying, "*Israel, who are you to be angry about me blessing Nineveh? That is what YOU were called to do. I have given you grace after grace, and how do you respond? Like a spoiled brat throwing a temper tantrum.*" Jesus later would use the parable of the "unmerciful servant" to illustrate a similar point. And that's the story of Jonah.

The Story of Jonah Applied

Just like Jonah, we sometimes can lose our focus. We can be more focused on our desires and interests. We can set ourselves up as king, and lose a proper view of the call.

We must be careful not to lose focus of the kingdom work in the world. It's bigger than your church or my church. Even though our churches are a part of the kingdom work, it's a small part. When we only focus on our little world, we begin to believe that this is all that matters. And if this is all that matters, then we are somebody special.

Ultimately, the world will begin to revolve around our lives and our perspectives. When this shift of perspective happens, we will lose focus of the kingdom work and we won't fully see the kingdom. If we develop a faulty view of the kingdom, we won't see who the real King is. And then we will become the king in our Kingdom--and Jesus will just be our servant.

I once heard Dr. Richard Ross preach one of the most powerful sermons I've ever heard on the supremacy of Christ. I asked for permission to share a section of that sermon with you and he enthusiastically agreed. He knows how important the following text is to us, as leaders. So, for the next several minutes you will not read one human word. The words you are about to read have their origin in the divine realm. God's word is powerful and effective. So, read carefully and, if possible, read it out loud in order to preach it to yourself. See if your view of Jesus doesn't change after this is over.

"In the beginning was the word. And the word was with God and the word was God. He is the image of the invisible God. By him all things were created, both in heaven and on earth, visible and invisible. Whether thrones or dominions or rulers or authorities all things have been created through him and for him. He is before all things and in him all things hold together.

Then God said, "Let us make man in our image whom I have created for my glory." But she took the fruit and she ate. And she gave some to her husband who was with her and Adam ate. Through one man sin entered into the world and death through sin. And so death spread to all men for all have sinned. And men began to multiple on the face of the land. All of us like sheep have gone astray. Each of us has turned to his own way. For all have sinned and fall short of the glory of God. And the wages of sin is death. The Lord will judge his people. It is a terrifying thing to fall into the hands of the living God. But God so loved the world that he gave his only son that whoever believes in him would not perish but have eternal life. Therefore, the Lord himself will give you a sign. Behold! A virgin will be with child and she will call his name Emmanuel. Christ emptied himself taking the form of a bondservant being made in the likeness of men.

And Mary gave birth to her firstborn son and the Word became flesh and made his dwelling among us. And the child grew in wisdom and stature and the grace of God was upon him. Now, from this time Jesus began to preach "Repent! For the kingdom of heaven is near!" Now after six days Jesus took with him Peter, James, and John and he led them up a high mountain. There, he was transfigured before them. His face shone like the sun and his clothes became as white as the light. A bright cloud enveloped them and a voice from the cloud said, "This is my son, whom I love. Listen to him."

Now the disciples came to him privately saying, "Tell us. What will be the sign of your coming and of the end of the age?" Jesus said to them, "This gospel of the kingdom shall be preached to the whole world as a testimony to all the nations and then the end will come. And they will see the son of man coming on the clouds in the sky with power and great glory. Then men seized Jesus and arrested him and took him to Caiaphas the High Priest. The High Priest said to him, "I charge you under oath by the living God. Tell us if you're the

Christ, the Son of God." "Yes! It is as you say. And in the future you will see the Son of Man sitting at the right hand of the mighty one and coming on the clouds of Heaven."

Then the High Priest tore his clothes and he said, "He has spoken blasphemy! We don't need any more witnesses! What do you think?" And they answered, "He is worthy of death!" And when they had come to the place, which is called the skull, there they crucified him. The Lord was pleased to crush him. Smitten of God. He laid on him the iniquity of us all. He himself bore our sins in his body on the cross so that we might die to sin and live to righteousness. Christ died for sins to bring us to God.

Joseph took the body and wrapped it in a clean linen cloth and laid it in his own new tomb. As it began to dawn on the first day of the week Mary Magdalene and the other Mary came to look at the grave. And behold! An angel of the Lord descended from heaven and came and rolled away the stone. The angel said to the women, "Do not be afraid, for I know that you are looking for Jesus who was crucified. HE IS NOT HERE. HE HAS RISEN!

Now, to the apostles Jesus presented himself alive after his suffering, appearing to them over a period of forty days. And he led them out as far as Bethany and he lifted up his hands and he blessed them. "You will receive power when the Holy Spirit comes upon you and you shall be my witnesses in Jerusalem and in all Judea and Samaria and even to the remotest parts of the earth. And after he had said these things he was lifted up while they were looking on. And a cloud received him out of their sight. He was clothed in a robe reaching to his feet and girded across his chest was a golden sash. His head and his hair were white like wool, like snow. And his eyes were like flames of fire. And God said, "Sit at my right hand until I make your enemies a footstool for your feet. God seated him at his right hand in the heavenly places far above all rule and authority and power and dominion."

Now, when the day of Pentecost had come and they were all together in one place and suddenly there came from heaven a sound like a violent rushing wind and it filled the whole house where they were sitting. Peter raised his voice and declared to them, "This Jesus God raised up again, which we are all witnesses. Therefore, having been exalted to the right hand of God and having received from the father the promise of the Holy Spirit he has poured forth this, which you both see and hear.

Therefore, let all the house of Israel know for certain that God has made him both Lord and Christ. This Jesus that you crucified!" Now when they heard this they were cut to the heart and they said, "What shall we do to be saved?" Peter said, "Repent, each of you and be baptized in the name of Jesus Christ for the forgiveness of your sins and you will receive the Holy Spirit."

The grace of God has appeared bringing salvation to all men instructing us to deny ungodliness and worldly desires and to live righteously and Godly in this present age, looking for the appearing of the glory of our great God and Savior, Jesus Christ. The Lord, himself, will descend from heaven with a shout, with the voice of the archangel and with the trumpet of God. And the dead in Christ will rise first. Then, we who are alive and remain will be caught up together with them to meet the Lord in the air.

And when the Son of Man comes in his glory and all of his angels with him then he will sit on his glorious throne. All the nations will be gathered before him and he will separate them, one from another. He will say to those on his left, "Depart from me accursed ones, into the eternal fire which has been prepared for the devil and his angels." Then the king will say to those on his right, "Come, you who are blessed by my father. Inherit the kingdom prepared for you from the foundation of the world." And there was a multitude no one could count from every nation, tribe, people, and language singing, "To him who sits on the throne and to the lamb be PRAISE and HONOR and GLORY and POWER forever and ever!"

Jesus said, "I am the way and the truth and the life. No one comes to the father except through me. Behold! I am coming soon. I am the alpha and the omega, the first and the last, the beginning and the end."

The next time we are tempted to make the ministry about us, we need to reread this section. Let it remind us exactly how majestic King Jesus really is. He is supreme over everything we could ever possess. He is glorious and precious. He is not some genie in a bottle that sits waiting to fulfill our requests. He doesn't work for us. He is sitting on the throne of the universe and we must recognize the extreme privilege it is to serve on *his* team. Yes, He is gracious. Yes, we can approach the throne with confidence. But this does not mean that we take His supremacy lightly. And God help us when we attempt, consciously or unconsciously, to have kids follow *US* instead of following *JESUS*. He will not share his glory with anyone. We must be careful to submit to his leadership at all times.

Maybe today you realize for the first time that you have been treating Jesus in an inappropriate way, and today you need to stop. Spend a moment now asking Him to forgive you and to help you to have a more clear view of Him from now on. 1 John 1:9 says, *"If you confess your sins, He is faithful and just to forgive you of your sins and cleanse you from all unrighteousness."* Thank Him for His forgiveness today.

Or maybe this new view of King Jesus is helping you to finally believe He is big enough to take care of your needs. Spend a moment now telling Him you will do what He asks you to do even if you don't see how He will provide. Tell Him you are willing to step out of the boat and trust Him with your life. As He says in Matthew 6:33, *"Seek first His kingdom and His righteousness, and all these things will be added unto you."*

Now that we know who the real Jesus is and have a proper view of the call and the caller, let's pray in response to what we have just seen and heard. Only Jesus can truly bless our ministries. The principles in this book are worthless without Him. Nothing trumps the favor of God on our lives. So, I challenge you to close this book, kneel at this time, and pray to King Jesus. Sit in His presence for a while. Then, get up and walk in victory!

CONCLUSION
CHAPTER 8

To conclude, if you implement the principles found in this book it should help you better communicate what your family ministry is all about. Your purpose statement and service times will probably be different than mine, but here is an example of how my team communicates our strategy when a new parent asks us to tell them about our ministry:

*"Hi! I would love to talk to you about our family ministry at Lakeside. Here at Lakeside, we are a family ministry that counts...literally! One, two, three, two, one. We have **one** purpose, helping kids connect to Jesus daily, weekly, monthly, and yearly. We do that through **two** major groups each week, big group and small group. We believe kids thrive best when they are involved in both a big group and a small group setting. Our big group times meet on Wednesdays at 6:15pm and our small group times meet on Sundays at 9:45am. So, we have **one** purpose, **two** groups, and **three** decisions we desire every student to make. We want every kid to meet Jesus, fall in love with Jesus, and serve Jesus. We also believe in prioritizing the **two** institutions God has established for discipleship, the family and the church. And the **one** major focus of everything we do is the person and work of Jesus Christ. **One** purpose. **Two** groups. **Three** decisions. **Two** priorities. **One** person. If you want to know more about our staff or any events we have coming up, visit www.lakesidebc.org. Do you have any questions or needs that I could help you with today?"*

Of course, this conversation doesn't always go exactly that way, but it is nice to have a "script" of sorts that our volunteers and staff can have on their minds so they will be prepared. Hopefully this book has encouraged you to think through how your team could answer the question, "Can you tell me a little bit about your church?"

It has been a privilege to walk through this journey with you. Thank you for spending time to read it. I hope this book has been beneficial for your ministry in some way, and I hope it has rekindled the passion you have for Jesus. Decide what parts of this book you will apply to your life, and let your creative juices flow with your own ideas for ministry. And stay connected with us as we continue the conversation at www.familyministrythatcounts.com.

We are always looking for new and innovative ideas for enhancing each part of our ministries. You can help other churches from around the nation by giving ideas on making big group meetings better, or managing small group ministries. What do you do to help kids meet Jesus (evangelism)? What about discipleship, helping kids fall in love with Jesus? How do you encourage and train kids to serve Jesus?

Please help us to create blogs and resource books as we strive to work in synergy to help more kids connect to Jesus daily, weekly, monthly, and yearly. Remember that ultimately our job, as ministry leaders, is to help kids connect to Jesus daily, weekly, monthly, and yearly through intentional relationships and strategic experiences so that they can meet Jesus for the first time, fall more deeply in love with Him, and begin to serve Him in every area of their lives.

APPENDIX

Recap Reading Experience

One Purpose: *Connecting Kids to Jesus Daily, Weekly, Monthly, and Yearly*

Life is hard. People are broken. Ministry is an attempt to help broken people become whole and whole people to become broken for broken people. Pastors are broken, too. We overcomplicate ministry because we want to please people. Because of this, we add more programs. But as we strip ministry down, we see that it is fairly simple. Ultimately, we have one purpose: to help kids connect to Jesus daily, weekly, monthly, and yearly. This purpose is simple, direct, and incomplete. It is not *how* we do what we do, but *why* we do what we do. It should help keep us focused as we calendar, budget, and execute the ministries God has entrusted to our care. It also implies that there will be more than one person connecting to Jesus.

Two Groups: *Community Requires Being Together*

Community is a biblical theme. Our environment should be set up in a way that makes it easy for kids to have community. Kids have to be together in order to have community. Kids thrive when they hang out in big group *and* small group settings. Big group will probably be the most effective hang out for inviting unchurched kids into the ministry. The goal of big group is to move kids to small group. The "win" for big group is not entertainment, but experience. The "win" for small group is not education, but relationship. *Education happens with the messages we teach in big group and small group settings.*

Community Requires Being Together in Big Groups

Big group experiences are important. They should be fun, energetic, and welcoming. They will most likely be the entry point for most kids. We evaluate our big group hangouts by asking three questions: (1) Is the environment appealing? (2) Is the presentation engaging? (3) Is the content helpful? Big group is where kids can hide so they can "come and see" before they get involved in a small group. The ultimate goal of our big group is to invite unchurched kids to embrace the gospel and to move them towards a small group.

Community Requires Being Together in Small Groups

Small group experiences are important. Our small group experience should give kids nouns. Nouns are a person, a place, a thing, and an idea. The *person* is the small group leader. Small group leaders should be present, create a safe place, partner with parents, make it personal, and move them out. The *place* should be safe and should be a physical, unchanging location. The *thing* is God's story throughout history. The *idea* is the vision kids should have from God on how their story fits into his story. It is our job to give kids a person, a place, a thing, and an idea!

Three Decisions: *Spiritual Formation Made Easy*

Spiritual formation is simply helping kids meet Jesus for the first time, helping them fall in love with him by getting to know him better, and helping them begin to serve him. We believe it starts with us, as pastors. What makes the Great Commission so "GREAT"? Jesus chooses to *let us participate* in God's story. He invites us in the same way he invited his original disciples: Meet me. Fall in love with me. Serve me. Evangelism was not the first thing on Jesus' mind. It was the climax, or the natural outcome, of his ministry. And as we go deeper with intimacy with Jesus, pray with passion for God's presence and power, build leaders for ministry, disciple kids to move toward maturity, penetrate the culture through relationships, and create outreach opportunities, we will see more kids meet Jesus, fall in love with Jesus, and serve Jesus for the rest of their lives. Now *that* is a life worth living.

Two Priorities: Church and Home

Influencing the Influencers: If we truly want to have a lasting impact with children and teenagers, we must realize that influencing ONLY kids is not the answer. We must influence the influencers. God ordained the family AND the church to be the primary means for discipleship in the world. Parents and volunteers are the influencers most capable of making a significant impact in the spiritual growth of the kids God has entrusted to our care. As leaders, we must constantly be looking for opportunities to train, inform, encourage, equip, and influence the influencers in order to maximize what little bit of time we have with our kids. Nothing is worth more than influencing the next generation for Christ. Legacies are born this way.

Appendix 2

Connect Four Strategy

Connect Four is an attempt to help us connect with Jesus at home and at church on a regular basis throughout the year. The challenges in the Connect Four strategy are broken down into daily, weekly, monthly, and yearly. Here they are:

- Connect with Jesus at home through his word *daily*.
  - o This means that we should strive to read his word daily. This really isn't that hard to do. If we want to grow towards maturity we must prioritize our time in scripture. Just give God one episode of your favorite show once per day and, instead of watching it, have a quiet time or listen to a chapter of the Bible on your Bible app.
- Connect with Jesus at church through his people *weekly*.
  - o This is extremely doable. Think about it. We should prioritize our church attendance anyway. So if we truly want to move towards maturity we should at least attend church once per week. That would equal four days per month. Maybe you can't make every Sunday, but chances are your church has other days of the week than just Sunday for you to find a worship service and small group. Make spending time with other Christians a higher priority than sports or other things. It will be worth it in the end.
- Connect with a mentor/accountability partner *monthly*.
  - o Few things are more important than accountable relationships with people you can trust. People who love you and are willing to speak hard truths into your life are people worth hanging out with.

Proverbs 27:6 says, *"The wounds of a friend can be trusted, but the kisses of an enemy are many."* The question you need to ask is this: do I want a true friend or a bunch of enemies? Most people only want to have "friends" that tell them how awesome they are. But according to this verse, a true friend is willing to tell you what you *need* to hear, even if it isn't what you *want* to hear. Accountability conversations look like this:

True Friend - "Do you want me to be your friend or your enemy?"
You - "I don't want you to be my enemy! I want you to be my friend."
True Friend - "Then what I am about to say might hurt your feelings, but know who it is coming from. I am your friend…"

Then the accountability partner will tell the person they are talking to what they observe in his or her life that needs adjusting. Make sense? The goal is to meet together monthly.
- Connect with Jesus through extracurricular events *yearly*.
  - This is where it gets fun. Choose a Christian concert or conference to attend. Go with your small group. Attend camp or a mission trip. When we say "extracurricular event" all we mean is an event that is not part of your churches weekly schedule. Your church probably offers fun events throughout the year. Let these events be one of your extracurriculars. The reason we encourage this is so we don't get

stagnant and routine in our faith. We need times when we can get a "shot in the arm" of spirituality. This is why prioritizing extracurricular events throughout the year is so important.

- Connect four people to Jesus along the way.
  o We will never grow to our full potential until we help others connect with Jesus. This might look like inviting one of your friends to an event designed to help them meet Jesus. It might mean you take one of these friends to an extracurricular event with your small group. It really could be as simple as sitting at the lunch table sharing the verse of the day from your Bible app. However we choose to connect our friends to Jesus we need to be in constant prayer for them. Lee Strobel often says, "Before we talk to our friends about God we need to talk to God about our friends."

Use the Connect Four strategy for your teenager, but also use it for your elementary kids as well. Begin early developing the spiritual disciplines of our faith. Encourage parents to go through the Connect Four Strategy with their children and teens, and encourage preschool parents to start developing spiritual habits so that when their child is old enough to participate they will already be in the normal routine of spiritual disciplines. Encourage a "new normal" for parents and tell them to "grow and tell". GROW closer to the Lord and consistently TELL their kids about what King Jesus is teaching them. Discipleship will be passed on more effectively when you use the Connect Four strategy and then GROW and TELL.

The Unreached People Group

One year, I was privileged to take a trip to Ecuador for a church mission trip. We took several adults, as well as a few teenage boys, with us. I remember one participant, Fran, who was in her early 60's. She was a sweet little lady who couldn't speak a lick of Spanish. She had never been overseas and had never really experienced a different culture. Still, the entire trip was amazing for her.

I remember the day we landed back in Houston. We were desperately craving American fast food and the sweet nectar of Heaven, Dr. Pepper. So we stopped for lunch.

As we were getting out of the van, Fran burst out in tears. Something really upset her, and we were trying to calm her down in order to find out what it was. She finally choked back the tears enough to say, "I can't take it anymore. They are just so negative to one another."

"Who, Fran? Who is negative to one another?" I asked. With tear-filled eyes, she looked towards two teenage boys who had been on the trip. "They have been talking bad to one another the whole trip. And I can't take it anymore."

I had to hold back the laughter. I had been around the guys all week, and never once saw them do anything different from what they had always done. They were really good friends and always seemed to have a good time together. They did what any normal teenage boy does with a close friend; they talked trash to each other.

Then it hit me. Fran had spent an entire week in a different country, engulfed in a foreign culture, and was unable to speak the language of the people. And not once did she experience culture shock. Yet, she had culture shock by spending one week with a few teenage boys. There's something unique about the teenagers we serve. They are a different breed of Homo sapiens.

This is why it is important to have a crash course in youth culture in order to better understand some motives behind this book. It is imperative for us to know our audience before we can effectively minister to them. It's essential to understand this sub-culture--and why we even do student ministry in the first place. (Did anyone ever notice that student ministry is nowhere in the Bible?)

I once heard a story about missionaries who traveled to Africa. They began having conversations with some people in a certain village, and they shared the Gospel story. The missionaries used the color black to represent sin and the color white to represent being cleansed of sin. The tribesmen shook their heads in disagreement. "No!" they said. "Black is clean!" The missionaries tried to explain the colors again, with no luck. It seemed, to the missionaries, that these men were under some voodoo-like spell, and they actually believed sin was good.

The tribesmen kept disagreeing with the missionaries until one man figured out what was going on. To a black tribesman in Africa, white represented being dirty--when the white sand from the land, or white ash from a fire, got on their skin. They would have to wash off the dirt or ash in order to be made clean. To them, white really did represent being dirty and black really did represent being washed clean. The story illustrates why it is always important to know the audience we are trying to serve before we reach out to them. If we misunderstand teens, we might jump to wrong conclusions and respond inappropriately to them.

Framing the Youth Culture

In his book, *Youth Ministry 3.0*, Mark Oestreicher helps frame the youth culture from its humble beginnings. Adolescence is a term that found popularity in the early twentieth century from a man named G. Stanley Hall. He taught that adolescence was the period between puberty and adulthood. When Hall described adolescence, he was talking about an 18-month period of time. In the early 1900s, the average age for the onset of puberty in girls was 14.5.[37]

> *Note: researchers who study the onset of puberty almost always study girls, because the signs are much more visually obvious with girls than with guys. Also, girls are more likely to talk about puberty than guys are. In fact, guys tend to lie about the whole thing! But researchers tend to agree that guys are most often a year or so behind girls in puberty and maturity.*[38]

Generally speaking, in the early 1900's, adolescence for girls began at age 14 1/2 and lasted until the age of 16, when the girl was considered an adult by society. So adolescence lasted for about 18 months. Fast forward to today. According to The National Center for Biotechnology Information: *"Adolescence begins with the onset of physiologically normal puberty, and ends when an adult identity and behavior are accepted. This period of development corresponds roughly to the period between the ages of 10 and 19 years, which is consistent with the World Health Organization's definition of adolescence."[39]*

I don't know if the changes for the age of puberty are due to better scientific methods, or whether there has been a change in the environmental conditions and diets of young people. Either way, adolescence has now been extended from eighteen months in 1900 to *at least* 9 years today. New brain research is suggesting that, cognitively speaking, it may last even longer. In 2006, Ronald Kotulak of the Chicago Tribune wrote:

> "Brain scientists like to joke that car rental companies must have the best neuroscientists because they won't let a person rent a car until age 25. But the real reason is clear to any actuary: Every year between 5,000 and 6,000 teenagers are killed in motor vehicle accidents and 300,000 are injured. Teen crashes are not just caused by showing off, substance abuse, aggression, and thrill seeking or speeding, although they play a role, said Jay N. Giedd. Recent research suggests that an important culprit is the immaturity of the teenage brain and its lack of multitasking skills--especially in boys. *The last part of the brain to mature is the prefrontal cortex,* Giedd said, *which may not fully develop until the mid-20s."* (emphasis added)[40]

So, according to Jay N. Giedd, chief of brain imaging at the National Institute of Mental Health child psychiatry branch, we can't expect teenagers to become full-fledged adults until their mid-twenties. In his book, *Teenology*, Jim Burns shares a stage of adolescence called 'Late Adolescence or Emerging Adulthood' (ages 18 to mid-20's). He says, "Today, parents are seeing their emerging adult children move back home and take longer to live independently...the issues that make up the adolescent years rarely are completed until the mid-twenties."[41] If these observations are correct, adolescence begins at the approximate age of ten, and doesn't fully end until the mid-twenties. That means the length of time for adolescence has jumped from eighteen months in 1900 to almost fifteen years today.

Why We Should Know This

Why are we looking at these statistics? We need to understand how much our society has changed in the past century. Not long ago, the term "teenager" was non-existent. Before the 1900s, you were either a child or an adult. There was no such thing as a youth culture. Therefore, student ministry was not even a twinkle in Jim Rayburn's eyes.

Some people say student ministry is unbiblical because the Bible never speaks of age segregating. Some would say student ministry needs to be abandoned due to the lack of scriptural references. And I would have to agree, to some extent, that we might have stepped a bit too far from the Biblical model of ministry in how we "do" student ministry today.

The Biblical model of any ministry is twofold: the family and the church. These are the two institutions God has established. And He established the family *before* He established the church. If what we implement doesn't somehow strengthen the family or the church, then we are doing something wrong. Too many student ministries have neglected the family, and even the church! Student pastors are often guilty of focusing only on those who meet the age requirements for student ministry. (I addressed this topic in chapter six)

However, to say student ministry is unbiblical is the same as saying a cowboy church or a biker ministry, or Celebrate Recovery is unbiblical, these ministries are designed with a particular audience in mind. There is always the danger of one of these ministries becoming separated from the universal body of Christ, but it does not mean they should be considered unbiblical.

A Case FOR Student Ministry

The reason student ministry is not mentioned in the Bible is because there was no youth culture for the Apostles to reach. Let's not forget that it wasn't until the era of Constantine the Great that official church buildings began to be constructed. Before this time, Christianity was considered illegal. Because of this, the idea of different ministries within a single church made absolutely no sense. Christians met in homes, private places, or even underground burial sites.

When Paul wrote to the church of Corinth, for instance, he was not referring to one congregation meeting in a single church building. He was writing to all Christians meeting in house churches or other places in the city of Corinth. He would refer to them as one church, but his writings would have been circulated from meeting place to meeting place until everyone had a chance to hear his message.

The goal of the early church was to meet together often, encourage one another, pray, meditate on the Holy Scriptures and the Apostles' teachings, worship the Lord, and spread the good news. They met as *families*. The congregants were few because the locations were small. There were no preschool and children's wings. There was no separate youth building to contain the wild, minion-like middle schoolers. There were no middle schoolers…#lucky

The point I am trying to make is that the early church, which happened to be the people to pen the scriptures, never had a youth culture to reach. Therefore, they never told us how to evangelize teenagers or how to do student ministry. That wasn't their focus at the time. But, they did have competing cultures that required uniquely different methods for spreading the Gospel.

The Apostle Paul spoke differently to the Jews than he did to the Gentiles. Why? Because these two people groups were distinctly different cultures with contrasting worldviews. Paul could start gospel conversations with a Jew by explaining the Messiah from the Old Testament scripture. However, he would have to start in a different place in human history for a Gentile to understand they even needed a savior. This is why Paul said: *"But we preach Christ crucified: a stumbling block to Jews and foolishness to Gentiles,"* (1 Corinthians 1:23) Paul knew that the two cultures needed the gospel explained to them in different ways and with different starting points. So, when he went about doing ministry work he had one mantra in mind. *"I have become all things to all people so that by all possible means I might save some. I do all this for the sake of the gospel that I may share in its blessings."* (1 Corinthians 9:22b-23)

When Paul was in Athens at the meeting of the Areopagus, he recognized the audience he was speaking to. In Acts 17:18-20 we read:

> "A group of Epicurean and Stoic philosophers began to dispute with him. Some of them asked, *'What is this babbler trying to say?'* Others remarked, 'He seems to be advocating foreign gods.' They said this because Paul was preaching the good news about Jesus and the resurrection. Then they took him and brought him to a meeting of the Areopagus, where they said to him, 'May we know what this *new teaching* is that you are presenting? *You are bringing some strange ideas to our ears*, and we want to know what they mean.'" (emphasis added)

Clearly, Paul was not talking to a group of Jews. He recognized this and decided to begin not with Jesus as the fulfillment of the Old Testament Messianic prophecies, but with the creation story. He started there in order to help frame their perspective of a creator God to whom they were accountable. For a people group who had no Biblical worldview, Christ being crucified was nonsense. They didn't understand the *need* for a Messiah, so they thought the whole story was foolishness. The Jews, however, stumbled over the crucified Lord because, though they believed in a Messianic figure, they had a different Messiah in mind.

Even though the New Testament never mentions teenagers or student ministry, you don't have to look far before you see the tension between cultures and the struggles, as well as transferable principles, the early church experienced as they strived to be faithful ministers of the message of Jesus Christ to every tribe and nation. I believe that if the Apostle Paul were alive today, he would be on the front lines of student ministry--because he would recognize the cultural differences, as well as the extreme potential, of this new tribe of people.

The Creation of a Subculture

From the moment our country began requiring kids to attend formal education and through the development of the public educational system, our society has developed this subculture called adolescence. What happened as a result of this cultural shift has been one generation after another, for the first time in history, hanging out with age-segregated individuals for the bulk of the day. The American landscape changed from having children and adults *only* to having children, *adolescents*, and adults. And the world began to view teenagers as "not-quite" adults. The new accessibility of college for more teenagers also extended the adolescent time frame from high school graduation to college graduation. And because of this new phase, which structured kids to hang out with other kids their age, the youth culture was born. And it is in full swing to this day. Now, we can fight against the culture and say, "This is not the biblical way!" Or you can remember this: You can't blame a lost person for acting lost. Andy Stanley once said in a sermon,

> *"We need to stop expecting outsiders to act like insiders while insiders act like outsiders."*

In other words, why are we surprised that our culture doesn't reflect Biblical principles? Most of our society might call themselves "Christians, but they wouldn't claim true allegiance to Christ. How can we expect them to adhere to His teachings? Plus, I believe culture only reflects the hearts of the people within that culture. By the way, what we are talking about here is an organizational issue. It is neither secular nor sacred. It is not a moral issue. It is "amoral," unconcerned with the rightness or wrongness of something. The way society chooses to structure itself changes with every generation. So we have to stop *blaming* society and start *understanding* it. Once we have a better understanding of our cultural context, we will be much more effective in reaching kids within that context with the good news of Jesus Christ. Now, *THAT'S* the ultimate goal.

Our current society has chosen to structure itself by requiring kids to attend buildings, called public schools that segregate them by age. They spend, on average, 8 hours per day/180 days per year in this new environment. They do this for at least 13 years of their lives. And this does not factor in extra-curricular activities. This means they spend 18,720 hours engulfed in age-segregated, big group and small group settings before they even graduate high school. This continues through college, although I didn't worry with including those numbers at this time.

Most middle schools today consist of 6th graders through 8th graders. If you haven't made the transition to welcoming 6th graders in your ministry, you might look at your local schools and mimic the age-segregation they choose to use. It will make integration into your church more natural for 6th graders and their families. If your city schools don't include 6th grade in their middle school, you should keep them in the children's ministry. But if the schools include them in the middle schools, I am a huge proponent of matching the school structures.

Either way, it's a good idea to have a transitional strategy in place for these 6th graders, as well as their parents. Developmentally, they are not quite adolescents yet. 6th grade is the beginning of puberty for many kids, but not all. Many churches have a separate department just for 6th grade kids. You may or may not be able to do this, but I would encourage you to figure out some way to start connecting with them. This may mean a separate Life Group or other Bible study just for them. There might be a parent who could lead this class. Maybe you plan a special outing or retreat each year, where you and some older kids could initiate them into the student ministry. Be creative and allow your student leaders to join in the planning.

If we have 6th through 12th grades representing our ministries, this means a student we aim to reach spends 8 hours per day, 180 days per year, for 7 years, in school before graduating your ministry. This equals 10,080 hours in the age-segregated environment. On the contrary, we will have the same student spend, at best, 2 hours per week, 45 weeks per year, for 7 years in our student ministry. BTW...these are generous numbers for the average student. The amount of time we have to influence them is around 630 hours. I'm not a math whiz, but 630 is a far cry from 10,080. Even if you are a super-pastor with fully dedicated teenagers spending twice as much time at church as the normal student, you won't even get close to the influence the society has on our teenagers.

One thing we can learn from these numbers is this: STOP WASTING TIME ON THINGS THAT DON'T MATTER! Sorry....I don't normally have random outbursts like that. My point is, we spend a lot of time on dumb things when we should be focusing on helping build relationships, which move kids towards faith. We need to look at how to maximize our limited time with teenagers to help foster these types of faith-building relationships. Understanding how society has structured itself helps us to see that student ministry is a MUST. Who else can reach this largely unreached subculture? We need to recognize that we are more than ministers. We are missionaries.

(Recap Reading Experience)

Understanding teenagers as a sub-culture helps us to frame the topics in this book. Teens live in a different culture and require culturally distinct methods in order to reach them with the Gospel. They spend most of their time in age-segregated, technology-saturated, big group and small group environments. Even though the early church didn't tell us how to do *student ministry*, they did give us transferable principles on how to be the church and how to reach different cultures with the message of Jesus. It is our job, as student pastor missionaries, to contextualize the Gospel for a new generation. This way, we make the timeless truths of scripture culturally relevant for a new, and largely unreached, people group.

(Scriptures referenced in chapter seven)

Genesis 12:2 - "And I will make you a great nation, And I will bless you, And make your name great; And so *you shall be a blessing;*" (emphasis added)

Genesis 22:18 - "In your seed *all the nations* of the earth shall *be blessed*, because you have obeyed My voice." (emphasis added)

Genesis 26:4 - "I will multiply your descendants as the stars of heaven, and will give your descendants all these lands; and by your descendants *all the nations of the earth shall be blessed;*" (emphasis added)

Genesis 28:14 - "Your descendants will also be like the dust of the earth, and you will spread out to the west and to the east and to the north and to the south; and in you and in your descendants shall *all the families of the earth be blessed.*" (emphasis added)

Acts 3:25 - "It is you who are the sons of the prophets and of the covenant which God made with your fathers, saying to Abraham, '*AND IN YOUR SEED ALL THE FAMILIES OF THE EARTH SHALL BE BLESSED.*'" (emphasis added)

Psalm 96:3 - "*Tell* of His glory among *the nations*, His wonderful deeds *among all the peoples.*" (emphasis added)

Psalm 105:1-2 - "Oh give thanks to the LORD, call upon His name; *Make known His deeds among the peoples.* Sing to Him, sing praises to Him; Speak of all His wonders." (emphasis added)

1 Chronicles 16:8-9 - "Oh give thanks to the LORD, call upon His name; *Make known His deeds among the peoples*. Sing to Him, sing praises to Him; Speak of all His wonders." (emphasis added)

Ezekiel 37:27-28 - "My dwelling place also will be with them; and I will be their God, and they will be My people. "*And the nations will know that I am the LORD* who sanctifies Israel, when My sanctuary is in their midst forever."" (emphasis added)

Ezekiel 39:7 - "My holy name I will make known in the midst of My people Israel; and I will not let My holy name be profaned anymore. *And the nations will know that I am the LORD, the Holy One in Israel.*" (emphasis added)

Psalm 67:1-4 - "God be gracious to us and bless us, And cause His face to shine upon us-- Selah. That Your way *may be known on the earth*, *Your salvation among all nations*. Let the peoples praise You, O God; Let all the peoples praise You." (emphasis added)

Sample Parent Council Expectations Form

Thank you for your participation in our Parent Council. I appreciate all you have done in the past and look forward to working alongside you in the ministry to our kids at Lakeside.

Here are a few expectations for serving on this council:

1. Lead with humility.
2. Meet with your ministry department leader three to six times per year for the purpose of calendar planning.
3. Be a sounding board for your ministry department leader on issues within the ministry.
4. Be involved in the ministry. Be willing to be called on to lead certain events/gatherings as well as help the church staff events with sponsors and other volunteers.
5. Participate in Parent Council group email messages periodically.
6. Be a conduit between parents and the family ministry team. Also, be a representative of the family ministry to other parents.
7. Promote unity within our family ministry and church.
8. Be willing to lay aside personal preferences for the sake of the overall health of the ministry.
9. Keep all meetings and conversations confidential.
10. Be willing to step down from the council in the event that life becomes too busy to continue involvement or if you find you cannot support the vision and direction of the family ministry.

Parameters for Calendar Scheduling

1. We are a ministry FOR THE FAMILY. Don't calendar too much or have too expensive of events.
2. Understand the different ministry seasons. Example: Fall might be "Outreach". Spring might be "Inreach". Summer might be Dirt Work. (In order for growth to occur you have to do dirt work.)
3. We will say "no" to GOOD things for the sake of the BEST thing. No sacred cows.
4. Whatever you suggest you have to be willing to do.

Everything we do must fulfill our mission statement: Connecting kids to Jesus daily, weekly, monthly, and yearly. Does what we do help kids meet Jesus? Or fall in love with Jesus? Or serve Jesus?

Appendix 6   149

Ministry Vision Worksheet

Scott Cormode, Fuller Seminary, defines vision as, "a shared story of
future hope." We will use this definition in our exercise here. Use the
questions in this worksheet to formulate your team's own vision.
Let's break down Cormode's definition to better understand how to
apply it to our ministry. We will need work backwards through the
statement.

• "...*future hope*"

    o This is the most important part of a vision. It
communicates, not what IS but what COULD BE. It is
what I like to call the "vision statement."

    o What do we *hope* our kids will do or be in the *future*?
(Mature, authentic, Godly, honorable, etc.)

        ■ _____
        ■ _____
        ■ _____
        ■ _____

    o What are the major priorities and core values our church
affirms? (The Bible, Evangelism, Discipleship, Worship, etc.)

        ■ _____
        ■ _____
        ■ _____
        ■ _____

    o How do we confine these thoughts into a single sentence?
        o Remember: this statement doesn't have to include
everything you do in ministry. It is more important
for it to be memorable than for it to be complete.

- Note: The sample vision statement for this book is, "Helping kids meet Jesus, fall in love with Jesus, and serve Jesus by connecting them to Jesus daily, weekly, monthly, and yearly." You should substitute this statement with your own statement when necessary as you read through this book. But notice how the statement is memorable and accurately communicates a future hope we have for all of our kids even though it is not complete. The statement is not meant to tell *HOW* we do what we do, just *WHY* we do what we do.

- *Your turn*: As a team, come up with a few different one-sentence statements that could communicate the "WHY" of your ministry. It should fit in the space provided below.

Vision Statement:

_____

Vision Statement:

_____

Vision Statement:

_____

Vision Statement:

_____

- "...*story* of future hope" For a "story" to be effective it must:
  o Be clearly articulated with no confusion.
  o Be able to be repeated with ease by the whole team.
  o Be specific on *certain* details necessary for accomplishing the vision statement.
  o Not be too specific on *nonessential* details that could overwhelm the hearer.
- How can your team craft a convincing story that accurately and clearly conveys the vision statement? ^(future hope)

  - Note: The sample "story" for this book is, "*We have one purpose, connecting kids to Jesus. We do that through two weekly groups, big group and small group. We desire every child and parent to be part of a big group and a small group. Big group is important, but small group is even more important. Big group meets on Wednesday nights at 6:15pm and small groups meet on Sundays at 9:45am. We want every child and parent that enters our doors to make one of three decisions: Either they need to meet Jesus for the first time, fall more deeply in love with him through discipleship, and/or begin to serve him in personal ministry. One purpose. Two groups. Three decisions.*"
  - This does not have to be your "story". I am just giving you an example of what I mean by "story". The "story" is the common vocabulary you and your team use to communicate "*HOW*" you plan to accomplish your "*WHY*". ^(vision statement)

- *Your turn*: As a team, discuss what details of your ministry must be included in your "story". Don't include everything. It will only confuse people. Look at your story through the eyes of a visitor. They just need the basic info. You don't want to scare them off by overwhelming them with nonessential information. Keep it simple.

  - *What is your vision statement?* (future hope)
    - _____
    - _____
    - _____
    - _____
    - _____

  - *What weekly programs do you have in place to lead kids to reach your vision statement?* (Big group, small group, etc.)
    - _____
    - _____
    - _____

  - *What do you want every student to become as a result of his or her time with you?* (Meet Jesus, fall in love with Jesus, serve Jesus, etc.)
    - _____
    - _____
    - _____
    - _____

  - *Now write out common language your team should use in order to consistently communicate the story.*

- ○ *Write out sentences you can all agree on and begin memorizing them.*
  - ▪ _____
  - ▪ _____
  - ▪ _____
  - ▪ _____
  - ▪ _____
- ○ *Practice saying them to each other.*

- "A **shared** story of future hope" For vision to stick it must be *shared* often. This is the common mistake most teams make. They spend time developing a great statement yet they never share it effectively. And they wonder why nobody is embracing the vision. *People won't embrace what they haven't heard. #communicate*
- Collaborate as a team how you can effectively and creatively share the vision statement and story often.
  - ○ What communication resource does your church have available? (Posters, printers, banners, digital and social media, etc.)
    - ▪ _____
    - ▪ _____
    - ▪ _____
    - ▪ _____
    - ▪ _____
  - ○ What communication platforms are your kids and their parents using daily? (Social media, podcasts, text blasts, etc.)
    - ▪ _____
    - ▪ _____
    - ▪ _____
    - ▪ _____
    - ▪ _____

○   Which people on your team will be responsible for
    weekly and monthly communication of your ministry
    vision?

    ▪   _____

    ▪   _____

    ▪   _____

    ▪   _____

    ▪   _____

Remember, vision is one of the most important aspects in any
ministry. Without vision your team will be like a ship without a
compass. You will just move from wave to wave with no clear
direction. You may get lucky from time to time and actually do
something significant, but it will just be that, luck. Instead, you
should be strategic in your efforts to make disciples. God expects his
followers to be engaged in the ministry he has entrusted to them. We
can't just go through the motions and expect great things to happen. It
starts with us being strategic and intentional in our efforts.

Endnotes

155

[1] Duhigg, Charles. *The Power Of Habit.* 1st ed. New York: Random House LLC, 2014. Print.

[2] Whitney, Donald S. *Spiritual Disciplines For The Christian Life.* 1st ed. Colorado Springs, CO: NavPress, 1991. Print.

[3] Lewis, C.S. *Mere Christianity.* New York, NY: Harper Collins, 1980. 199

[4] Stanley, Andy. *Making Vision Stick.* Grand Rapids, Michigan: Zondervan, 2007. 19, 21

[5] Miller, Donald. *Blue Like Jazz: Nonreligious Thoughts on Christian Spirituality.* Nashville, TN. Thomas Nelson Publishing, 2003.

[6] Busby, Dave. *The Heart of the Matter.* Published by Riverside Group, 2009. Pg. 21

[7] Stanley, Andy. *Deep and Wide: Creating Churches Unchurched People Love to Attend.* Grand Rapids, Michigan: Zondervan, 2012.

[8] Haddon Robinson, *Biblical Preaching,* (Grand Rapids: Baker Academics, 2001), 20.

[9] Stanley, Andy. *Deep and Wide: Creating Churches Unchurched People Love to Attend.* Grand Rapids, Michigan: Zondervan, 2012. Pg. 190

[10] Joiner, Reggie, Kristen Ivy, and Elle Campbell. *Creating a Lead Small Culture.* Cumming, GA: Orange, 2014. Pg. 18

[11] Ross, Richard. *Student Ministry and the Supremacy of Christ.* Bloomington, Indiana: CrossBooks, 2009. Pg. 37

[12] Oestreicher, Mark. *Youth ministry 3.0: a manifesto of where we've been, where we are and where we need to go.* Grand Rapids, MI: Zondervan, 2008. Pg. 107

[13] Strommen, Merton, and Richard Hardel. *Passing on the Faith: A Radical New Model for Youth and Family Ministry.* Winona, MN: Saint Mary's Press, 2000. Pg. 39-40

[14] Oestreicher, Mark. *Youth ministry 3.0: a manifesto of where we've been, where we are and where we need to go.* Grand Rapids, MI: Zondervan, 2008. Pg. 107

[15] Joiner, Reggie, Kristen Ivy, and Elle Campbell. *Creating a Lead Small Culture.* Cumming, GA: Orange, 2014. Pg. 29

[16] Ibid., Pg. 33

[17] Ross, Richard. *Student Ministry and the Supremacy of Christ.* Bloomington, Indiana: CrossBooks, 2009. Pg. 37

[18] Joiner, Reggie, Kristen Ivy, and Elle Campbell. *Creating a Lead Small Culture.* Cumming, GA: Orange, 2014. Pg. 172

[19] Coleman, Robert E. *The Master Plan of Evangelism.* 2nd ed. Grand Rapids, MI: Revell, 1993.

[20] Ibid., Pg 21

[21] Ibid., Pg 38

[22] Ibid., Pg 40

[23] Ibid., Pg 64-65

[24] St. Clair, Barry. *Jesus-Focused Youth Ministry.* Stone Mountain, GA: Reach Out Youth Solutions, 2002.

[25] Joiner, Reggie, and Kristen Ivy. *It's Just a Phase, So Don't Miss It.* Cumming, GA: Orange, 2015.

[26] Wright, Steve, and Chris Graves. *reThink: Decide for yourself. Is student ministry working?* Wake Forest, NC: InQuest Publishing, 2008. Pg. 81-83

[27] Joiner, Reggie, and Kristen Ivy. *It's Just a Phase, So Don't Miss It.* Cumming, GA: Orange, 2015. Pg. 54

[28] http://theologicalmatters.com/2016/10/04/less-traditional-student-ministry-might-mean-more-disciples/

[29] Joiner, Reggie. *Think Orange.* Colorado Springs, CO: David C. Cook, 2009. Pg. 87

[30] Kimmel, Tim. *Connecting Church and Home.* Nashville, TN.: Randall House Publishing, 2013. Pg. 1

[31] Kizer, Darren, Christine Kreisher, and Steph Whitacre. *The Volunteer Project: Stop Recruiting. Start Retaining.* Atlanta, GA.: 181 Publishing, 2015. Pg. 3

[32] Joiner, Reggie, and Kristen Ivy. *It's Just a Phase, So Don't Miss It.* Cumming, GA: Orange, 2015. Pg. 56

[33] Kizer, Darren, Christine Kreisher, and Steph Whitacre. *The Volunteer Project: Stop Recruiting. Start Retaining.* Atlanta, GA.: 181 Publishing, 2015. Pg. 33

[34] Ibid., Pg. 42

[35] Ibid., Pg. 53

[36] Ibid., Pg. 54

[37] Oestreicher, Mark. *Youth ministry 3.0: a manifesto of where we've been, where we are and where we need to go.* Grand Rapids, MI: Zondervan, 2008. Pg. 31-32

[38] Ibid., Pg. 130

[39] *Canadian Pediatric Society. "Age Limits and Adolescents." The National Center for Biotechnology Information. November 2003. Accessed June 1, 2016. http://www.ncbi.nlm.nih.gov/pmc/articles/PMC2794325/.*

[40] Kotulak, Ronald. "Teens at the Wheel: A SPECIAL REPORT." *Teens Driven to Distraction*, March 24, 2006, 2. Accessed June 1, 2016. http://www.illiniwest.org/pages/uploaded_files/6_driven_to_distra_due 9_10.pdf.

[41] Burns, Jim. *Teenology*. Bloomington, MN: Bethany House Publishers, 2010. pg 58

Author Bio

Preston is a veteran ministry leader and has experienced local church ministry as well as several Para-church ministries. He currently serves as Student Pastor at Lakeside Baptist Church in Granbury, TX. He also serves as Super Summer Evangelist at Super Summer Evangelism Training Camps for Texas Baptists. In addition to this, he also leads Ministry Cue, a ministry designed to provide resources and retreats to ministry leaders in an effort to help leaders get their cues from King Jesus.

Over the years, he has served in many different roles with the Evangelism Department for Texas Baptists. Before this, he traveled the nation full-time for three years as a coordinator for evangelism outreach events.

He holds a Masters degree in Christian Education and will be awarded a Master of Divinity degree from Trinity Theological Seminary in Evansville, IN. by the end of 2018.

He lives with his wife, Sarah Dee, and kids Perry, Titus, and Parker in Pecan Plantation, TX.

Made in the USA
San Bernardino,
CA